FIBROMYAL

The Support Effect.

By Peter J Atkin.

© May 2018 Peter J Atkin.

All rights reserved.

No part of this publication may be reproduced in any form or by any means, including scanning, photocopying or otherwise without prior written permission of the copyright holder.

Disclaimer and terms of use. Any perceived slights of specific persons, peoples or organisations are unintentional.

This book is not intended as medical advice.

The information contained herein is intended solely for general information of the reader.

The information here is not intended to diagnose health problems or to take the place of professional medical care.

All content is for general information purposes only.

FIBROPARTNERS
THE SUPPORT EFFECT.

The journey of understanding and mutual support

Contents

About the Author 4
Introduction... 5
Living with Fibromyalgia a partners account...................... 8
Understanding Fibromyalgia. 11
Why do I need to understand Fibromyalgia? 15
It's Not You, It's Fibro 22
Fibromyalgia Pain 27
The Fibro Flare... 33
Fatigue 41
Fibro Fog (Cognitive Dysfunction) 46
Emotions: 54
Depression.. 63
Part Two 66
Fibro - Lynn's Story 66
Unhelpful Behaviour V's Supportive Relationship 67
Helpful Supportive Behaviour 72

Accounts from others with fibromyalgia.................................76

20 Useful tips to help each other 80

Caring for your partner..93

Communication is the key. 97

Communicating fibro to others. 102

Terminology help page...107

Summary 111

Moving Forward. 113

Inspirational Quotes 114

Useful Products. 117

A MESSAGE TO PARTNERS..118

Dedications and acknowledgements......................................119

About the Author

Firstly, Peter is not a medical expert and makes no claims to be. The contents contained in this book are in no way intended as medical advice and should not be treated as such.
Peter is the partner of a fibro sufferer.
His partner Lynn has fibromyalgia. They have known each other for sixteen years and have been a couple for eleven of those
Peter has spent the years with Lynn, reading about fibro, talking and more importantly listening to Lynn to understand fibro and how to support her in managing the condition.
He spent two years training as a life coach and this undoubtedly has helped him in supporting Lynn. It not only helped him to support Lynn but also taught him how to deal with the issues and feelings he had with fibro and also to help others.
The best way to support your partner is by trying to understand them and what they are going through on a daily basis and helping them to 'manage' their symptoms. The aim of this book is to put the training and experience Peter has to good use in helping other partners to understand fibro and how to deal with the issues and feelings that both of you have to manage.
He is simply sharing what he has learned, putting his coaching skills to good use and sharing his experience of fibro and how to manage it as a partner to offer some help to those that are having difficulty understanding it.

Introduction

Anyone living with this devastating illness will be all too familiar with its long list of symptoms: chronic pain, debilitating fatigue, cognitive dysfunction, anxiety and depression to name but a few.

It attacks the strongest of people without sympathy or remorse. It shows no mercy as it eats away at your life

Education is the Key.

A common problem for those with Fibro is the lack of knowledge that surrounds them, in order to help, in addition to the book Fibromyalgia The Support Effect, an in depth guide to managing Fibromyalgia for partners and family, we have produced a short handy guide that all the family can easily review to get everyone involved in learning a bit more, breaking the ice over worrying issues to help when communication can seem difficult.
Download this FREE Partners and Family Guide to Living with Fibromyalgia.

http://bit.ly/FREEpartnerfamilyGuide

Fibromyalgia: The condition is invisible. The effects are anything but. It can ruin your career, your social life, destroy your relationships and create disharmony within your family. It has the potential to make day-to-day living unbearable, if you let it.

Having fibromyalgia is not a choice but you can choose how you live with it.
I wrote this book, as the partner of a fibro sufferer to help and guide others through the stress and strain of living with the illness. Consider it your 'fibro partner'.

I am not a medical expert but someone who has years of experience of learning about and understanding the effects of fibro, not just on the person with it but also their loved ones.

The book is written in two parts, the first part is based on my life as the partner of someone with fibro. The second part is an insight into Lynn's story, the person who has it. The changes it made to her life, how she sees life now and the positive changes she and we as a couple have made to live life to the best with this terrible condition.

The purpose of this book is to help the person with the condition, their partners and family to achieve the best life possible with fibromyalgia. It is focused on helping loved ones understand what the one with it is going through and how to deal with the emotional effect's it has on your partner providing simple explanations and simple do's and don'ts, to help you understand and be the support your partner needs. This book also explains what actions we have taken both as a couple and as individuals; to lessen the impact fibro has had on our life and vastly improve our quality of life with fibro as the third party in this complex 'ménage et trois'

It is not about complex medical terminology and what fibro may or may not be, it is a simply written book about understanding and managing fibro, based on research, experience, listening and not being afraid to accept and deal with the challenge's fibro presents. All content is based on what we, as a couple have tried and tested during our thirteen years together.

There have been many trials and tribulations, things that have worked, things that haven't, good days and bad days but Lynn my partner is not a quitter, she has a positive attitude and will not let fibro beat her.

Lynn is not afraid to try new things, taking things one step at a time but she still has bad days, the difference between then and now is that her bad days are fewer, further apart and not as devastating.

"Sometimes the smallest step in the right direction ends up being the biggest step of your life. Tip Toe if you must, but take a step." – Naeem Callaway

"

This book is focused on the positives, the things that have worked for Lynn and for us as a couple.

"You can't be cured but you don't have to be beaten."

Living with Fibromyalgia
A partner's Account

To see my loved one so enveloped by fatigue so she can hardly move is soul destroying. I have witnessed Lynn for days lying on the sofa, wrapped in bandages to ease the pain and no matter how much comfort I tried to give it never helped.

I am lucky. I don't have fibro. Only one of us has it but we both have to manage it, we are, after all partners. I wish I could take the pain away and own it for her but I can't. What I can be is the best support possible.

Being the partner of someone with fibromyalgia can be difficult and demanding. It is a very misunderstood condition; the symptoms don't just affect the one with it but has a knock-on effect on those around them. This is my account, from someone looking in on fibro and how watching the woman I love so much suffer the pain she suffers on a daily basis makes me feel. One of the many thoughts I keep in my head is "No matter how bad it makes me feel, it is worse for Lynn." Fibro has to be one of the most frustrating conditions for a partner to witness and deal with.

Frustration in not being able to take away the pain no matter how much I want to. I would gladly sacrifice my health to at least share the pain with Lynn and give her some time off. Fibro is relentless, it doesn't come and go, it is ever present but in varying degrees of intensity.

I felt as I am sure many partners do, completely useless. I didn't know how to support her; I didn't understand this thing called fibromyalgia.

I didn't understand why one day she was happy and loving, the next day snappy, moody and distant.

One day Lynn would be passionate and sexy, another day completely disinterested in me. It would have been easy to think I had done something wrong or she didn't fancy me anymore. It is very easy to allow fibro to cause you to doubt yourself.

Lynn describes fibro as: a gremlin on her back, constantly hurting her whenever it pleases, reaching into her body and pulling on her tendons and tissues as if she were a puppet and the gremlin was the puppet master.

I wish I could grab hold of the invisible little bastard, pull it off her and donate it to science to find a way of destroying it and the rest of its kind which infect the lives of others.

I couldn't do that obviously but what I did decide is to learn as much as I possibly could about this demonic condition and be the best support I could possibly be for my partner.

I have spent the years with Lynn, studying, talking to her and more importantly listening to her to learn how fibro affects her and what I can do to help.

It is so easy to turn a blind eye and hide behind the belief that it will go away with the help of a few pills and a bit of rest. It is effortless to blame the one who has fibro for having it and tell them to 'get a grip.' (One of the things you should never, ever say to someone with fibro). There are some cruel comments made to fibro sufferers and people with other chronic conditions, which I am sure, are associated with a lack of understanding. What I would say to those who don't understand is;

> *"Imagine how you would feel if you had to deal with the effects of fibro,*
> *what would you want from your partner?"*

It has taken years of personal research and being with Lynn to reach the level of understanding I now have and I will no doubt continue to learn with every day that passes. Being the partner of someone with fibromyalgia is at times challenging but the relationship with Lynn is always rewarding. My training as a life coach has undoubtedly helped me and I am happy to say, been of help to friends who have partners with chronic conditions. People from all over the world contact me through Fibro partners to seek and offer support, ask questions and share experiences. There is currently no cure for fibro but until there is, understanding and support are so very important in managing it. Don't be afraid to talk about it, share feelings and most importantly, listen.

Understanding Fibromyalgia.

"Behind every chronic illness is just a person trying to find their way in the world. We want to find love and be loved and be happy just like you. We want to be successful and do something that matters. We're just dealing with unwanted limitations in our hero's journey."
— Glenn Schweitzer

What is Fibromyalgia?

Those who suffer from it will know exactly what it is but do you, the partner, know what fibro is?

The medical term for fibro is, according to British Medical Journal:

Summary points

- Symptoms of fibromyalgia are chronic widespread pain associated with unrefreshing sleep and tiredness
- Fibromyalgia is not a diagnosis of exclusion and often occurs in patients with other conditions, such as inflammatory arthritis and osteoarthritis
- No clear pathophysiological mechanism for fibromyalgia has been established, but evidence suggests that there is an abnormality in central pain processing
- Diagnosing fibromyalgia can allow the patient's polysymptomatic distress to be explained, thereby reducing fear and doubt

- Fibromyalgia has no cure, but a range of drug and non-drug treatments can reduce symptoms and their impact on the patient's life
- Trial evidence for all forms of treatment in fibromyalgia generally shows only small to moderate average effects

Most doctors—particularly rheumatologists, pain specialists, and general practitioners—are familiar with patients who describe chronic pain all over the body, which is associated with a range of other symptoms including poor sleep, fatigue, and depression. This complex of symptoms is sometimes referred to as fibromyalgia. Management of patients with this condition is often complex and challenging. The diagnosis of fibromyalgia has long been controversial, with some experts questioning whether it exists as a separate entity.1 However, the symptoms and distress experienced by patients with fibromyalgia are real. The causes of fibromyalgia are incompletely understood, and optimal management is compromised by the limited evidence base for the available treatments. This article reviews current thinking about what fibromyalgia is, whether it is a useful diagnosis to make, and which drugs and non-drug treatments can be used to treat it.

Got it?
Thought not, don't make it easy, do they?

Lynn's description:

"Fibro is an annoying frustration that is always there, inside me. It causes pain, like I have never experienced before, negative thoughts, like I have never experienced before and relentless fatigue. Every day something happens to my body or mind that feels like an alien reaction to what I thought was Lynn, a pain, a thought, that

I never used to have. It is as though my body actually hates me at times and is a complete separate entity from the person I am in my head. It's like I'm constantly carrying a gremlin that physically feels like a bag of wet sand, heavy and relentless, hanging around on my shoulders that hurts me wherever and whenever it chooses; it feels like it reaches into my body, grabs a handful of tendons and does it's best to pull them out through the back of my neck. It's like being a puppet and fibro is the sadistic puppet master! Fibro causes me intense, unforgiving pain and fatigue as I'm constantly trying to figure out that one thing I can do to make me feel that little bit better, what can I eat, drink, do that will lift me out of this state for just a few simple hours or even minutes. You get to a point in the cycle where you feel in stasis, but you have to remember that things have to change, you can't stay feeling like this forever and my favorite saying, *'It will Pass'*

Think that sums it up a bit clearer doesn't it?

Fibro is without doubt a very high maintenance, complex and difficult to understand condition. There are so many different symptoms that affect different people in different ways. However, there are also many generalizations' in symptoms that are common to those with the condition. I can only speak from personal experience and pass on what I have learnt so that it may be of help in understanding.

As a partner remember:

    You don't have fibromyalgia. Your partner does.

                    But:

Together you can manage it.

For me the first step in understanding fibro is accepting that your partner has it. Neither of you like the diagnosis you have been given but you do have to accept it to be able to move on. You need to accept that things will change. You can either, withdraw and hide behind the false belief that it can be cured with a bit of rest and a few pills or you can learn about it, understand it and help manage it. You are important. Your understanding and support can make living with fibro a whole lot better and more tolerable for your partner and trust me on this one, being there for them also makes you feel a whole lot better about yourself.

Why do I need to understand Fibromyalgia?

Understanding is probably one of the most important tools in managing fibro. The lack of understanding can lead to lack of support and that can make it a whole lot worse, not just for your partner but also you. The benefits to both of you are equally as incredible. Learning about and understanding how you can help your partner can make such a major difference to the quality of both your lives.

The following diagrams are intended to illustrate two different perspectives on understanding and support.

Cycle 1

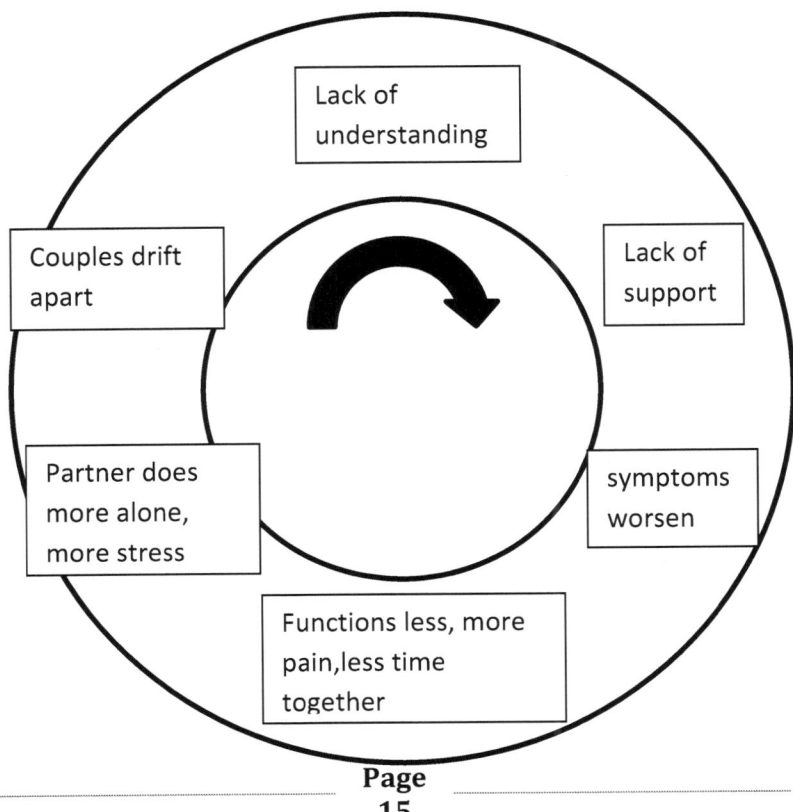

As you can see it is a vicious circle that keeps spinning around and around, going nowhere, gathering momentum, until like your life it eventually spins off its axis out of control and lands up who knows where? Lack of understanding doesn't just mean one person can carry on as normal and nothing changes. It has a knock-on effect.
Fibro can be a very lonely condition to have. Because it is an invisible illness, those who have it tend to suffer alone, it is not like other visible conditions which are seen and it is recognised that support is needed. On the outside someone with fibro appears 'normal' with no apparent condition. However, on the inside they are suffering, it can be a struggle just to keep going some days. I liken them to a swan on the lake, gracefully gliding along on the surface but beneath the surface, paddling furiously just to keep going.

The pain associated with fibromyalgia is physically draining; it causes fatigue, depression, cognitive dysfunction. Without support and understanding it is easy to withdraw into a shell, doing ones best to cope, this can cause great stress, the main cause of 'fibro flares' (which is talked about in a later chapter.)

Constant stress will cause symptoms to worsen. With the persistence or worsening of symptoms comes the lack of function, everyday chores that would once be seen as easy, become difficult, they take their toll on the body and on the mind as the person with fibro struggles to understand and comprehend what is going on to have such a debilitating effect. When the body is tired fibro takes its opportunity and will strike, this can cause a major 'flare' unless the signals are noticed and the body is rested. This is without doubt going to have a massive effect on your life together; the one with fibro feels less like doing the things you normally enjoy doing together, socialising, and hobbies, whatever your interests are. Lack of libido is also a common side effect of fibro, especially when that person is unsupported. Understanding the knock-on effects is so important; if you as the partner acknowledge these effects, you can make changes to ensure rest and relaxation is an important element of your partner's daily requirement to be able to provide the energy needed for good times together.

A lack of understanding can lead to one partner, (the one who doesn't have fibro), doing more things alone or with others instead of working together to find new ways of doing what you love. Try new things together to create new, good memories and see that life really is what you make it.

The quality of life you once enjoyed as a couple needs nurturing and developing as failure to grow and build will stagnate the time together and diminish your enjoyment together as a couple, gradually you, as a couple may even drift apart.

Cycle 2

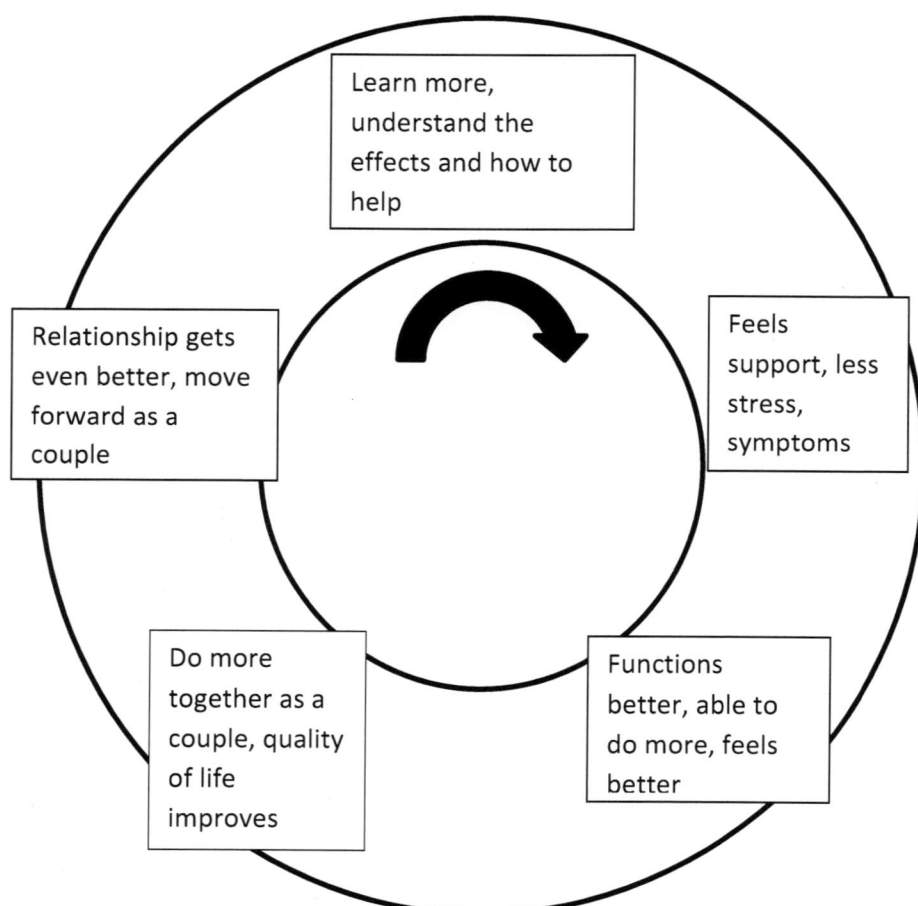

This is more like the wheel of a car which you are in full control of. You are moving forward all the time, going at your own speed on your journey as a couple, gathering knowledge, understanding and a happier life together.

It's not rocket science!

I say that because even though fibro is a complex condition which twists and turns, it changes and throws you curved balls, just when you think you have it under control something changes, a trigger surfaces to cause pain. ('Trigger' being something that causes a reaction in the body.')

When I say "It's not rocket science" I'm not talking about fibro itself.

What I mean is:

Taking the time to learn about fibro and giving support, WILL benefit all concerned.

Take the time to learn about what fibro is how it affects the person with it and what you can do to help. Trust me when I say, it is worth the effort! For someone with fibro, knowing they are understood and supported is a major factor in reducing stress, the main cause of 'flares'. The less stress the more the severity of symptoms reduces. The less severe the symptoms are, the more the one with fibro feels able to function. The more able to function the more quality time you will have.

All in all, a better quality of life for all concerned.

> Sometimes being understanding is more important than being right... Sometimes we need not a brilliant mind that speaks but a patient heart that listens... Not keen eyes that always see faults but open arms that accept... Not a finger that points out mistakes but gentle hands that lead!

I cannot stress enough how important understanding what fibro is and how it affects not only the person with it but those around them also.

Understanding comes with knowledge, with knowledge comes power, the power to combat the effects of fibro and enjoy life to the fullest, despite it.

Read, research and most important, listen.

Read: medical journals written by experts, these can be quite confusing if not written in simple terms rather than medical jargon but contain a wealth of information.

Read: Books like you are reading now, written by people who have personal experience of fibro, these are by far the best way to learn, there is no substitute for experience. Books like this contain an absolute wealth of information, not just about the condition itself but what works, tried and tested methods, routines, products, all learned from experience. Utilise the experience of others to gain the knowledge you need to understand.

"The only source of knowledge is experience." Albert Einstein

Research: Google is always a good source of research but again the best source of information is from those who have experience of the condition, don't be afraid to reach out to these people, ask questions of them and join online webinars and forums that have been created by those who have personal experience of fibro and successfully manage it. Lots of information can be found on our website www.fibropartners.com

Listen: the person with the most knowledge of fibro who without doubt is the one who has it. Listen to what they say, believe what they say, and don't doubt what they say. The reason why our relationship is so successful, the way we combat fibro and live a full life is because we both listen to each other. I listen to Lynn explain fibro and how it makes her feel, she listens to my concerns and feelings, we communicate!

"Communication to a relationship is like oxygen to life, without it....it dies" Tony Gaskins.

(Motivational speaker, author and life coach)

It's Not You, It's Fibro

As the partner of someone with fibro, it is often very easy to feel like you are always doing something wrong. There are many contributing factors in our partner's behaviour that can cause us to ask, "What have I done wrong now?" or feel like saying, "I'm sorry am I boring you?"

If your partner suddenly goes quiet or gives you a short, snappy answer to something you have asked, it probably isn't anything you have done wrong, it is more likely they are in pain and feel unable to respond to you whilst they are coping with that pain. Pain is one of the symptoms studied in greater depth in a later chapter of the book.

Are you boring them? Another symptom of fibro is 'Cognitive dysfunction', described in more detail in a later chapter.

This can cause your partner to suddenly drift off and stop listening to you or suddenly change the subject as they have suddenly remembered something from earlier.

One of the aims of this book is to help you understand that the sudden quiet spells your loved one drifts into, the sudden changes in mood and the anomalies in behaviour that cause you to question yourself, the sometimes silly and selfish way we can feel and the self-doubt that can be associated with living with fibro, is sometimes nothing to do with us as a partner and all to do with fibro as a condition.

The methods in this book work for my partner Lynn and I. The difference in the quality of life we now have compared to when we first got together as a couple is simply amazing. We will look at how to change negative thoughts into positive actions.

Remember:

When you are feeling unloved, not fancied or ignored:

It's not you, It's fibro.

Everyone's experience of fibro is unique to them, I can only write from the viewpoint of the partner of a unique woman who happens to have a condition called fibromyalgia. I can only use my own experience and understanding as a guide to help you understand the effects of fibro and support your partner.

The emotional relief of knowing that you are understood and supported can make a big difference to how a fibro sufferer feels.

Stress is a major aggravator to fibro, if your partner knows you are there for them, understanding and supporting them this will definitely reduce the stress.

To understand fibro, the most important thing to grasp is: It is not in your partners head. It is not imaginary or psychosomatic. It is however, in their brain.

Research suggests it is a chemical imbalance in the brain, some recent research suggests it may be an electrical imbalance in the brain.

Whatever it may be, it is real. The pain is real, the fatigue is real. The effects of fibro are real.

The second most important thing in my opinion is belief.

Believe your partner, when they tell you they are having a bad day even if they don't look ill.

Believe what they tell you, when they describe how they feel, even if it doesn't make sense to you.

Believe that it is fibro that causes mood swings, lack of libido, fatigue, depression, anger.

It's not you, its fibro.

Believe in yourself. Fibro is a devious little demon who can, if you let it cause la great deal of self-doubt.

For example: She doesn't fancy me anymore? What am I doing wrong? Why is she angry with me?

These are just some of the negative thoughts that can enter your mind.

We will deal with these in more detail later but for now and I say it again believe in yourself.

It's not you, its fibro.

What I would like to do in the following chapters is go through the symptoms of fibro and how we deal with them.

I say we not I because we are a team, Lynn and I manage fibro together. Communication is in our opinion the main priority in managing fibro. It has definitely helped us immensely and without it we would probably not still be going so strong and getting stronger by the day.

Don't automatically assume you are in the doghouse because your partner is ignoring you, quiet around you or appears 'in a mood' with you.

The chances are that the change in mood is nothing to do with you it may be because your partner is in pain, having an episode of brain fog, suffering from chronic fatigue, feeling depressed or in the midst of a 'flare'.

This is the time you need to draw on your reserves of self-assurance, strength of character and don't doubt yourself.

Do not feel sorry for yourself, instead feel supportive, the more support you can be, the quicker the episode will pass.

Fibromyalgia Pain

"I don't want my pain and struggle to make me a victim. I want my battle to make me someone else's hero."

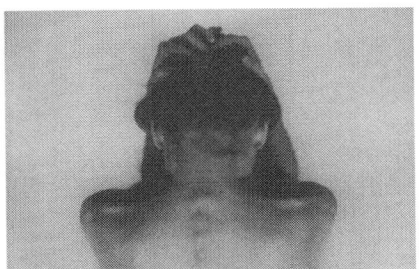

One of the main symptoms of fibro is pain, not just any pain but chronic widespread pain.
The definition of 'chronic pain' is a pain that has lasted longer than three months. By widespread, it is meant that the pain is felt in many areas of the body. The pain can be worse in one specific area than another but often will be chronic in all areas. So, chronic widespread pain is pain that can occur all over the body which has lasted longer than three months (according to the definitions). In my language, chronic widespread pain means it bloody well hurts all over, all of the time! The intensity of the pain varies but the thing I have to remember is that it is always present, it doesn't go away, and it just varies in intensity.

To be diagnosed with fibro there are eighteen separate trigger points of pain that are identified. That is an awful lot of pain that people with fibro have to deal with.
I always try to imagine how that must feel and put myself in my partners' shoes.

Imagine if you go to the gym and do an intense work out or over exert yourself, the next morning, you will no doubt hurt; your muscles will ache or feel like they are on fire. This is how someone with fibro can feel every morning without having done anything.

Do remember, someone with fibro has greatly increased sensitivity to pain. A bit of well-meant concern goes a long way. With fibro, pain is usually worse in the mornings when first getting up. Here is a 'don't'. I never ask anymore "how are you?" first thing in the morning. If Lynn has had a bad night the question just focuses her mind on how she is feeling and makes her feel worse. I simply look at Lynn's eyes and watch her body language to know how she is feeling. If her eyes are dull with no sparkle, her movements are sluggish and difficult, I know she is feeling 'not best ever' so I deflect by giving her a big smile tell her I love her or say something cheerful and complimentary like, "ey up sexy" and ask her if she wants a cup of tea and let her come around in her own time with space and a bit of peace and quiet. If her eyes are sparkly and she has a spring in her step I know it's a low pain day and she has woken up feeling pretty good.

Types of Fibromyalgia pain

Hyperalgesia:

Hyperalgesia is a condition in which the actual pain level is higher than normal. The thing to remember with people who have fibro is that they are far more sensitive to pain than those of us that don't have it. With fibro the brain seems to amplify the pain signals to the body.

For example, if I fell over and banged my knee or my arm, I would probably feel mild to moderate pain, Lynn would hurt like hell!! Here's a do/don't moment: Don't say, "Oh stop making a fuss that can't have hurt that much" or something similar, it's little comments like this that actually cause pain, emotionally

Allodynia:

Allodynia is increased sensitivity to touch or temperature. Things that wouldn't normally get a pain response in me do get a pain response in Lynn. It's like having severe sunburn without any visible signs of it, so sometimes a simple touch can hurt. A well-intended hug can hurt; even a kiss that's planted with a bit too much enthusiasm can hurt. Something as tactile and affectionate as stroking Lynn's arm or leg while sat watching a film, can feel like I am giving her a good rubbing down with rough grade sandpaper. I have learnt to start gently in whatever we are doing (especially that! yes I can guess the first thing that popped into your head then!)

Thermal Allodynia:

Thermal Allodynia is an increased sensitivity to temperature either cold or hot. For a fibromite, it means in cold weather they can't get warm for hours and the cold can physically hurt. What I would class as chilly can feel like severe frostbite to Lynn. At the other end of the scale, the suns heat can cause problems, the rays can actually hurt and the sunshine feels like a blinding light to the eyes. To manage this, in winter as I mentioned earlier, I buy Lynn good thermals and dish out plenty of warm cuddles at home to get her warm, I am in winter, her hot water bottle. In summer if we are going anywhere for a day out, or picnic by the river etc. then I make sure we have shade available or take a sunbrella or similar with us. There are small UV protective beach tents that can be bought for the kids which do a great job.

Wind breaks for days on the beach if there is a chilly sea breeze blowing. It's a matter of planning, just giving a little more thought to weather conditions.

There are other areas of pain that Lynn experiences which are common in those with fibro, which are:

Tension in head and neck:

Lynn uses products such as Volterol heat rub on the back of the neck or what she has found very effective is a product called magnesium oil spray. Lynn did some trials on this for a local company (whom we would highly recommend) and has had great results with it and uses it to this day. You could also buy your partner one or more of these products which work for Lynn: a neck massager, heated shawl, instant heat pads which you apply to the area that is aching, memory foam neck pillow for when sat watching TV.

I also learned how to give gentle massage which is a great way to ease the pains and relax your partner.

Back Ache:

A good product you could get your partner is a heated mattress for your bed, also a heated blanket/throw for when sat watching TV or just sat relaxing (or trying to) Again, what works is learning how to give gentle massage to work out any knots in the muscles caused by tension. When driving a lumbar support helps.

Knees:

Products such as Volterol and magnesium oil work well. A great thing to have is a triangle shaped support pillow which your partner places under the back of the knees when lying down, which also helps with lower back pain. Support bandages on the ankles to help maintain good blood circulation and helps keep feet warm.

Feet:

Buy your partner a foot spa and use it with Epsom salts to help relax the feet. Ankle supports help. You can also buy small heat pads which feet comfortably under the soles of the feet.

Hands:

Support gloves are a big help, they fit snuggly and support the fingers (course they do I hear you saying, that's why they are called support gloves, sorry I couldn't think of how else to describe their benefit) What also helps are wristbands which give the feeling of warming the blood circulating to the hands.

Fibro is a high maintenance condition, it is very complex in the different effects it has on different people. To manage it takes a great deal of thought and understanding, by both partners. Lynn as with all those with fibro, will have good days when the pain level is relatively low and bad days when it's a bitch and knocks her off her feet, otherwise known as a 'fibro flare'

Remember, people with fibro feel the pain more than those who don't have fibro, be sympathetic, believe your partner, if they say it hurts it's because it hurts and not that they are being over dramatic.

The main thing to remember about fibro pain is it is always present; it does not go away it just varies in intensity. Some days are low pain days which we class as good days and think of just one thing we would both enjoy doing, some days are bad days when pain levels are high and activities are out of the question.

Remember, body language is a good indicator of what sort of day it is going to be, a spring in the step, sparkly eyes indicate that it could be a good day. If the eyes are dull and movements slow and difficult then this would indicate a bad day.

Be prepared to adjust your day accordingly, show patience and empathy, do not criticize if plans have to change at short notice, pain does not always give advance warning of when it is going to strike.

What we need to remember when dealing with fibro pain is not only that it is always present but also that people with fibro are hyper-sensitive to the causes of pain.

The brain amplifies the pain signals it sends out to the body.

The Fibro Flare

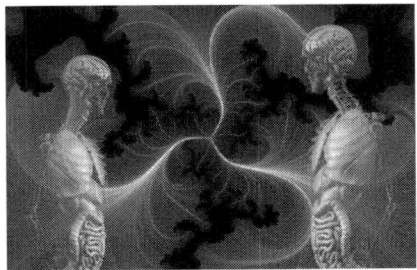

"You can't calm the storm, so stop trying. What you can do is calm yourself. The storm will pass." – Timber Hawkeye

What is a fibromyalgia flare? A flare is the worsening or exacerbation of symptoms that already exist. A flare-up is essentially the body's way of saying it is not coping. They can last for hours, days, sometimes weeks. Flares can be brought on by different things that we wouldn't notice.

Stress is probably the granddaddy of fibro-flare triggers and can cause the longest and most intense flares. In the early days before we were a couple I remember Lynn lying on the sofa for days wrapped in bandages with major fibro-flares, due to stress caused at that time by an abusive husband who ridiculed and criticized her because of fibro. Needless to say he got divorced! I obviously don't know what causes stress in your partners but I have learnt what stresses Lynn.

One way I have found to reduce the incidents of fibro-flares is to identify the things that cause the greatest stress and take on the responsibility for dealing with those things.

I reassure Lynn that they are being dealt with and deal with them. Petty arguments or bickering is a great cause of stress and the cause of unnecessary flares. We have found that communication is the key and a far more effective way to settle any differences we have. Over the years we have learned the art of successful communication and an actual 'argument' is virtually unheard of in our relationship. Yes, we have differences of opinion and disagreements but it is the way we deal with them that has made all the difference. What to us non fibromites would seem like the simplest of daily routines can cause stress, such as one of the kids forgetting to take the bins out, the kitchen being left in a mess at night and other things we might consider insignificant. By just thinking about what stresses Lynn and dealing with it beforehand I can reduce the daily stresses on Lynn and so far, it works. Lynn does still have flares but they are less intense, less often and don't last as long.

There are numerous factors or conditions that can bring on 'a flare'

On the following pages are some of the causes of flares and how they can be avoided or managed.

The Weather

Cold damp weather conditions are the worst. Lynn is like a barometer, she can tell when the weather is about to change when fibro pain starts to increase. When the weather starts to change and go colder, I go out and buy Lynn a couple of sets of thermal leggings and tops. Lynn is a country girl and loves the outdoors, trying to keep her indoors would be impossible, so best thing is for her to keep warm. Other things that help when the weather is really cold, wet, damp etc. is do the outside chores that your partner doesn't feel up to doing. I don't mean take over completely, Lynn like many others with fibro wants to do as much in the way of usual daily chores as she can and would get rather frustrated with me if I behaved like a mother hen constantly fussing. I make a point of asking, "Is there anything I can do outside" things like sweep up, take bins out, anything. Lynn will always tell me what she does or doesn't feel up to doing. Again, communication is the key. I also keep an eye on how long we have been out; if I start to feel the cold chances are Lynn is feeling it more. Ask the questions, "are you warm enough, have you had enough of being out here, do you want to go back home?" Again, the trick is communication with a balance of caring without 'fussing' too much.

Overdoing it

It's easy when Lynn is on a roll of good days of low pain to push herself that bit too hard and end up crashing into a flare up. To counteract this without being a mother hen is the difficulty I found. Lynn as I am sure many others do pushes herself to see how much she can do. As she says "I won't know my limits until I reach them" she has a point but sometimes the temptation is to push beyond the limits and that's when the dreaded 'Flare' descends. I have found in this situation the most supportive thing I can do Is, 'butt out' and let her get on with what she wants to do. Lynn more often than not will know when she has done enough. However: I do watch her body language and if she is obviously getting tired or the sparkle disappears from her eyes, I will simply ask "done enough yet my love?"

If Lynn is getting tired then the term 'done enough' registers with her and she rests.

Or

If her face is grimacing in pain but with stubborn determination she is carrying on I will use deflection and ask her to help me with something else less demanding.

Or

Go and make her a cup of tea and initiate a break in what she is doing.

Lynn is now wise to my little deceptions and spots when I am attempting them and will simply give me a smile and say something like, "okay I know, I've done enough for now" or " I am okay I just want to finish off what I am doing" and although she knows what I am doing she does appreciate the fact I care enough to watch out for her.

Travelling.

Travel seems to seldom be easy for someone with fibro and even what we would consider the easiest of trips can sometimes cause a flare. This may be because the trip involves one or more flare triggers, such as Disruption in sleep routines, fatigue, weather/temperature changes and stress. When we go on trips I make sure we have rest stops planned into the journey, so that Lynn can stretch her legs, walk around, have a cuppa etc. I also (having learnt the hard way for Lynn) is plan the journey in normal awake hours not overnight journeys. I say learnt the hard way because (and this is a perfect example of what NOT to do when planning a trip);

We went on holiday overseas, first one for a few years it was a last minute booking. The flight was on a Sunday night at just before midnight and was a four-hour flight. We had been away four years earlier and Lynn had managed a similar flight time okay. (during the daytime) The plan was, have a nap in the afternoon, get to the airport, have a relaxing wander round the shops, a bite to eat and then we would be boarding the plane and off on our holidays. The afternoon nap didn't happen! The airport shops had closed three hours before we got there, it was Sunday! The eating establishments were all closed, it was Sunday! The only place open was the bar, so we sat in the bar and Lynn had a couple of large vodka & cokes, (Lynn doesn't usually drink more than a small vodka or a small whiskey) Lynn spent four hours napping (or trying to) on the plane, in a cramped area because it was a last-minute booking we couldn't pre-book seats with extra leg room. The plane was cold and there were no blankets available. The result was Lynn (poor love) spent the first three days of the seven- day holiday in bed with horrendous migraines and fibro flare, requiring visits to the local medical practice for injections and treatments.

Many key ingredients for a flare were present in the end.

Stress, (no shops or cafes open) disruption to usual sleep pattern, (night flight), fatigue and temperature change (not being able to have restful sleep due to cramped conditions and cold plane with no blanket)

So, my friends a lesson learnt, next holiday is getting booked in advance with extra leg room seats, a daytime flight when shops are open, a blanket in the hand luggage in case it's cold on board and no necking large vodkas before we go.

It's all in the planning!

Lack of sleep or changes in sleep routine:

Getting quality, restful sleep is often difficult for those with fibro and whenever sleep is disrupted or there are changes to normal sleep patterns (if there is such a thing with fibro) a flare can develop. From a partners' perspective it is one of those things that we have to learn to deal with. Lynn goes to bed when she is tired which can be 10pm or even earlier. It is something we as partners have to accept.

If there are dishes left to clear up etc. then I just get on with things and make sure everything is ship shape so Lynn isn't greeted by a disaster area the following morning. It's little things like this, taking care of the everyday things your partner doesn't feel up to doing that makes all the difference.

Individual Sensitivities:

People with fibro are often extremely sensitive to certain things like, light, smells, noise which may trigger a fibro-flare. Lynn's main one is smell, especially perfumes, deodorants or flowers. We all know what kids are like with those, especially teenagers who love to bathe themselves in the stuff. Our two have to spray themselves somewhere away from Lynn in a well-ventilated area (sounds like the warning on a can of spray paint doesn't it?) We have found that these sensitivities can change, for example: I always used to come home with a bunch of flowers for Lynn every couple of weeks, as she loves fresh flowers but since the holiday migraines and flare up Lynn has developed a real sensitivity to fresh flowers, they bring on a migraine, especially Lilly's which are her favorite.

With this particular 'trigger' it's about identifying what sensitivities your partner has and avoiding them. That's all we as partners can do to help. Also touching on fibro fog which is in a later chapter, I do remind Lynn from time to time if I see her putting a particular spray in the supermarket trolley that has been a real trigger in the past and it has slipped from her memory.

There are other triggers I have read about such as treatment changes, illness or injury and hormonal changes. These are all individual to each person and all we can do as partners is deal with each one if and when they arise and support our partners.

TIP: Although it's not possible to prevent all fibro-flares it is possible to reduce the likelihood of them. You can do this by doing what Lynn does. She takes a few moments to write in a log what she has been doing each day, any changes in routines or products she uses. She logs when she has flares. That way she has learned to identify what the main causes of her flares have been and what to avoid.

Do's and Don'ts

Some Do's and Don'ts we have found very useful:

Do: be calm and compassionate, your partner will benefit from your calm. The best way for someone having a flare to allow it to pass more quickly is to be calm and relaxed about it, this will help.

Don't: start asking what could have caused the flare, during the flare, wait until it has passed before discussing possible causes.

Do: Let your partner rest, allow them time to recover

Don't: Constantly or periodically interrupt their rest asking them how they feel, has it passed etc. Your partner will tell you when it has passed. As Lynn says whenever she is experiencing a flare "It will pass".

Do: Listen to them, they know what will help them best. Ask only one question, "is there anything I can do to help" then listen and act on their request, it will most likely be simply, leave me alone for a while.

Don't: Fire suggestions of distraction at them, "shall we do this, will that help, if we did this it might help" etc. Again, it's all about communication, it is the key to managing fibromyalgia.

Remember; the symptoms of fibro are always present, they do not go away. A 'flare' is not something new; it is when the ever present symptoms suddenly worsen they flare up. Flares will happen, we can't make them disappear completely but we can help reduce the frequency and severity of them by identifying the main triggers. Triggers may not be the same for everybody, people react to different things in different ways but some triggers are common in fibro, stress being the main one.
The most effective way of reducing flares is to first identify and log when they happen and what you were doing prior, what was different, a different fragrance, a different routine, change in weather an event that caused anxiety or stress. A good thing to have is a log book specific to fibro such as the one Lynn uses.

Fatigue

"Resting is not laziness, it's medicine!" – **Glenn Schweitzer**

Fatigue is considered to be the second most common factor of fibro. Not just tiredness but overwhelming fatigue, to the point that the person with fibro feels they just simply cannot function. I think of it as how I would feel if I ran a half marathon full of 'man flu', let's be real here people, man flu alone is bad enough but the thought of even trying to run a half marathon with it is enough to send the fittest of us scurrying under the bed sheets!! The thing that we non fibromites have to remember is that even what we would consider the simplest of tasks, such as hanging out the washing, the weekly grocery shop or washing the car, can leave someone with fibro feeling like they have done the half marathon with man flu.
Sometimes the fatigue can come on immediately after the physical exertion, the following day or even a couple of days later.

Here is a don't moment.

Don't, say something like "you can't be tired already, you've hardly done anything"

Don't, accuse them of 'being lazy'

The fatigue that comes with fibro has other knock on effects such as 'fibro fog' which we will deal with in the next chapter.

Muscle tiredness, affecting the speed at which a person with fibro can do things, simple things again which we take for granted, walking the dogs or just walking.

Lynn cannot always walk at my pace, sometimes she can for a while but has to slow down or stop. Some days she walks faster than me. It all depends on how much effect fibro is having on any given day. On the days when fatigue prevents her walking at the same pace, I simply slow down and walk at Lynn's pace, it's a pleasant walk not a race. Does it matter if the walk has to be shorter than planned or you have to turn back sooner than you planned? Does it matter if it takes longer to get where you are going?

Don't – say something like "hurry up, we'll never get there at this rate"
Don't – get frustrated at having to slow down or speed on ahead and wait for your partner to catch up.

It is a misconception that pushing to increase the amount of exercise will help someone with fibro get fitter and build stamina. Pushing too much will undoubtedly just result in a major fibro flare. Don't push your partner to do more, the only person who can dictate the amount of exercise someone with fibro can do, is the person with fibro. Lynn has learned to listen to what her body is telling her, if she feels tired she will have a twenty minute 'power nap' that usually works and she wakes up feeling refreshed and able to tackle something else.
She may have one or two power naps in a day, she may have more, whatever it takes.

Coping skills also include relaxation and meditation cd's just lying down for twenty minutes listening to one of these really helps.

Again, it's about communication. Lynn listens to her body, I listen to Lynn. It's also about consideration and understanding.

If I was feeling lousy and absolutely shattered with man flu, I would want someone to help me with the everyday chores that needed doing, so when Lynn needs help, I help, it's that simple. I can hear some of you shouting at the book," I work all day, I am tired when I get home after a hard day" Here's a thought, take your worst day at work, imagine how that feels, imagine on that day, nothing went right, you couldn't accomplish whatever it was you were trying to accomplish, the frustration at not being able to complete what would normally be some simple task because you were just too tired to function. Imagine, what a crap day that would be. Now, imagine feeling that way day in day out with only a few good days thrown in. That my friends, is how fibro can feel on a daily basis due to fatigue.

Nobody said it was going to be easy living with fibro and having to consider so many different ways fatigue can affect your everyday life. No matter how difficult it is for me I always try to imagine how difficult it is for my partner Lynn who has the dreaded condition.

Fatigue can also have a negative effect on your social life. It helps to adopt a very flexible approach to social events. There will be times when social arrangements have to be cancelled at the last minute. Sometimes no matter how much Lynn has tried to plan rest periods into the day so that she will be able to attend social functions in the evening, it just doesn't work out and she is just too fatigued to attend. Don't make it a problem, no matter how bad you feel at letting friends down at the last minute, your partner probably feels worse. Friends who understand Lynn's condition know it's unavoidable when it happens, so it's no big deal to rearrange things for another time and if it happens again then it's no big deal to rearrange again. My attitude is that if it does ever become an issue to anyone then it is their issue, Lynn comes first, friendships second.

What also helps fight the fatigue is a good routine at bed time. Lynn's routine is, a warm shower, gentle rub down with fragrance free warming oils or magnesium oil.

In bed have an electric blanket on, wear ankle supports and what does really help is a 'Lumie light' which slowly reduces in light with a relaxing ambient sound to gently empty the mind of all those busy thoughts and hopefully lead to a restful night of quality sleep.

What I as a partner have learned to accept is that life with my beloved Lynn has to be lived at a slower pace, Lynn finds it difficult to slow down but she has had to learn and accept it. Lynn has learned to be okay with saying no sometimes and I have learned to be okay with being told no sometimes. This doesn't mean to say life will be unexciting and uneventful, it still is because, as Captain Picard of the USS Enterprise would say we 'have made it so' (one for the Trekkies out there). It's all about planning and prioritizing.

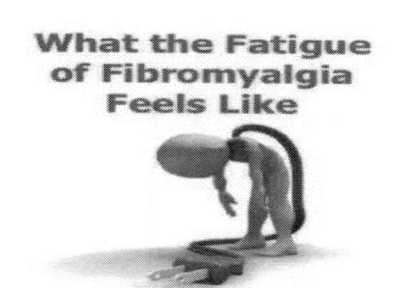

What the Fatigue of Fibromyalgia Feels Like

Remember: people with fibro have limited reserves of energy; activities that do not take up much energy in a person without fibro can be exhausting to someone with it.

Be aware of the limitations that fibro places on the person who has it, understanding the 'spoon theory' is a good way to remain aware.

Here's something for the person who doesn't have fibro to try: from the moment you wake up start counting spoons, one for waking up, one for getting dressed, one for washing and cleaning your teeth, one for preparing your breakfast, one for driving to work, get the idea? Every single act you carry out, make a mark on a piece of paper or in a notebook then at the end of the day count how many spoons you have used, you will be amazed at how many!

Don't be critical of rest periods, they will be more often but necessary, a person with fibro needs to rest when they feel tired to replenish their reserves of energy, to keep 'pushing on' is not going to help and may result in a dreaded fibro flare.

Be aware, be supportive.

Fibro Fog (Cognitive Dysfunction)

"Please be patient with me. Sometimes when I'm quiet, it's because I need to figure myself out. It's not because I don't want to talk. Sometimes there are no words for my thoughts." – Kamla Bolaños

Brain fog, also called fibro fog. The medical term for it is 'cognitive dysfunction'
This is one of the most common complaints of people with fibro. For many, it can be severe and can have just as big an impact on their lives as pain or fatigue. Some people say brain fog is more of a disability than their physical symptoms. Fibro fog is something that can be extremely frustrating especially if in their previous life before fibro, like my partner Lynn, they had high powered jobs that required them to multitask, to have excellent memory recall, required them to speak in public with clarity and other such qualities that fibro has deprived them of. Lynn does sometimes get frustrated with it but has come to terms and can see the funny side of it.

Having a sense of humor about it really does help by reducing the stress associated with frustration. As Lynn says, "If I didn't laugh about it, I would cry sometimes" Lynn's description of Fibro Fog is:

"It's like I'm struggling to find my way through a thick fog, trying to carry out a conversation but unable to find the word I need to use or forget what I'm talking about mid-sentence.

Quite frequently I will walk down the corridor to ask Pete a question and by the time I have got there I have forgotten what it was I wanted to say. One of the things I love about Pete is, when we are having a chat with other people, he will if and when necessary caringly interject and discreetly correct me. I know in my head what I want to say but it will not be verbalized that way, I will say something like ater patkin instead of peter atkin. I can be talking to my friend Vicky laughing about something our friend Tammy did but I will refer to her as Vicky because it's Vicky I am talking to.

Fibro fog is the thing that bothers me most, I can cope with pain but the confusion is a difficult one. I am/was a typical 'type A' person, a Project Manager for a business consultancy which required a great deal of mental alertness. Now I find it difficult to have the mental agility to get my breakfast ready if I am in the midst of a fibro fog attack.

It's a good job Pete has a fantastic sense of humor and ends up making me laugh, especially when I put my mobile phone in the fridge and walk into the office with the milk in my hand, it was very funny watching Pete trying to make a call with a carton of milk.

Fibro Fog Symptoms

Symptoms of brain fog can range from mild to severe. They frequently vary from day to day, and not everyone has all of them. Symptoms include;

- Word use & recall. Difficulty recalling known words, use of incorrect words, slow recall of names.

- Short-term memory problems. Forgetfulness, inability to remember what's read or heard.

- Directional disorientation. Not recognizing familiar surroundings, easily becoming lost, and having trouble recalling where things are.

- Confusion & trouble concentrating. Trouble processing information, easily distracted, forgetfulness of original task when distracted, and multitasking difficulties. Inability to pay attention to more than one thing.

The effects of fibro fog are about the only thing that cause Lynn to question her sanity, well that and the fact we have 6 terriers, 3 horses, 5 ferrets and probably a partridge in a pear tree hiding somewhere, which causes me to question my sanity.

What can a partner do to help with Fibro fog?

The thing I have found essential with fibro fog is patience. Getting frustrated because you can't understand what's being said to you because the words are a bit jumbled or wrong words are used is not helpful. A bit of patience goes a long way.

A Don't is; don't immediately try and finish off the sentence for your partner, this can be more frustrating for them as it's bad enough that they can't finish what they are trying to say themselves without you butting in and pre-empting what they are trying to say especially if you get it wrong!

Give your partner time to finish what they are saying, if Lynn can't remember she will say so, then I will ask "do you mean?" or "I know what you're saying"

It's a case of listening more closely to what is being said and the context of the conversation so you can understand what is being said not only in a conversation between the two of you but also with others.

Help by being her awareness.

Notice when your partner is struggling, as Lynn puts it, she may be 'lost in space' or numb to her surroundings.

For us we use a prearranged signal for Lynn, if she is struggling with a conversation when we are in company, she will touch my arm, which is my cue to help out. It is visibly frustrating to watch her struggling with memory loss and lack of concentration.

Making lists, even for things that may not seem important to you is one way that someone suffering from fibro can help them feel in control of what's happening around them.

Lynn will make up a list the night before of things she wants or needs to do the next day, things that non fibromites take for granted and will remember simple things like; ring mum, go to supermarket, and pick up prescription. What is also important to her is that she spends some time thinking of all the good things that have happened that day and being grateful for her day. By doing this she is reminded that not everything is about fibro and life is good.

This may seem 'over the top' but it is extremely likely that by the next morning unless they are written down simple things will be forgotten about.

When Lynn has a doctor's appointment, we will talk about what issues she wants to raise, questions she wants to ask and discuss what it is she is expecting from her doctor. I will either go to the appointment with her or if I can't Lynn will take a notebook with everything written in. It's a good idea to log the visits and the outcomes so you have a record of what's been said/done. The same applies to medication, have a designated medicine box and a diary of what meds have been taken at what time, any side effects, how the meds worked, that way you can help your partner find the right balance of what works.

One symptom that doesn't seem to affect Lynn to a great extent is directional difficulty; if anyone gets lost going anywhere it's me. Lynn usually ends up giving me directions.
Forgetting where things are is probably something, we all do, with fibro it's an added frustration. A good idea is having designated places for things and don't swap things around, keep continuity in where things are kept.

Something which can be frustrating for a partner (remember! what is frustrating for you is likely to be more frustrating for the fibro sufferer) is the inability to concentrate and be easily distracted. Sometimes I will be talking to Lynn and she will suddenly be distracted by something on tv and completely ignore me for a moment or change the subject to what's on the tv, then she will forget what we were talking about or just wander off. This can be annoying and frustrating, especially if it is something important you are discussing.

This is an area where patience and understanding are so important. Don't be offended by this behavior, you are not being ignored. What you have to say is not being regarded as unimportant; it is simply that your partner is in the midst of a fibro fog.

It isn't helpful to press your partner to continue the conversation, if it can wait then let it wait.

If it is something that needs to addressed there and then, bring the conversation around gently, not with a sharp "excuse me I was talking to you" I simply pause for a moment and then say something like "any way my love as we were saying" and give her a cheeky smile or a laugh and Lynn will either laugh with me and say "oh yeah sorry about that" or she will just say "sorry I'm not with it, if you think you are getting listened to now you are wasting your breath" and we will laugh about it and leave it until later.

Recognizing signs of 'The Fog'

The obvious ones are the appearance of not paying attention to anything you are saying, not listening to you and ignoring you. I say 'the appearance of' because that's how it appears but not necessarily true. Your partner may not appear to be listening when in fact they are doing their best to concentrate on what you are saying but it just isn't registering with them.

Remember: It's not you, It's fibro.

Body language is a good one, I look at Lynn's eyes, if they are bright and have a lovely sparkle to them I know it's a good day and the sun is shining and Lynn's mind is fog free.
If they are dull and tired then it's a foggy period (could also be that pain and/or fatigue are present). Only you know your partner well and can recognize when they are on good form or feeling under the weather.

As with the other symptoms of fibro it's about communication, ask your partner to tell you when they are feeling 'not with it' and fibro fog is having a field day. The answer I got to that one from Lynn was "of course I will my love, if I can remember to tell you"
Which, sort of proves the point that observation and paying attention to your partner's mood, body language and general demeanor is an important part of managing the invisible gremlin that is fibro. Yep, the other important tool in the box with fibro fog is a sense of humor!!

Fibro Fog

I came, I saw, I forgot what i came for.
I retraced my steps
I got lost on the way back
Now i have no idea whats going on

Remember: no matter how frustrating it can be for you when your partner seemingly ignores you or changes the subject for no apparent reason, it is more frustrating for the person experiencing it. Be kind, be patient, be helpful and supportive, do not criticise or ridicule them. If you both have a good sense of humour then use that to deal with fibro fog, Lynn and I share many laughs at the things said or done.

Emotions:

Fibro has a major effect on your partners' emotions. The big three emotions caused by fibro are; Anger, frustration and guilt, which can lead to depression.

Anger

"Be soft. Do not let the world make you hard. Do not let pain make you hate. Do not let the bitterness steal sweetness. — Iain S. Thomas

Anger is something we all feel, not just people with fibro, but with fibro there are more contributory factors that cause anger. It's commonly caused by the other 2 major emotions, frustration and guilt but also caused by other factors when fibro is involved.

I can only repeat that I am commenting on what Lynn and I experience and the general emotions common to many fibro sufferers. Your partners will have their own issues which cause anger. Only you can work these out. All I can say is it involves an informed decision. Do you tell yourself, don't ignore the anger or walk away and leave your partner to deal with it alone, or do you do just that? Sometimes that is the best solution, your fibro partner may just want some alone time and quiet space. The key is communication, ask the question, "do you want to talk about it or do you want some you time alone" There are of course times we get angry with each other when one does something to aggravate the other, this is general anger or annoyance not specific to fibro, again it's down to communication, asking why?
What is causing the anger?

Some anger issues are specific to fibro. Lynn describes what makes her angry most is how unfair fibro is; simply getting through the day can be a mental challenge. She so wants to contribute to be productive and make a difference not only to her life but that of her family.
Anger from the frustration of not being able to do the job she used to do and enjoy. The anger of this loss, the grief of a lifestyle lost and having to start again, learning how to 'get a life' with fibro for company has without a doubt proved very tough for Lynn to come to terms with.

How can I help my partner deal with this anger?

What works for Lynn is an imaginary STOP button in front of her and when she feels angry, she presses it (not physically of course, people would think she was a bit strange) anyway, she presses the imaginary button and takes a moment to think about why she is feeling angry and what is just one thing she can do to make her feel better. When she is angry, I simply ask "will pressing the stop button help?" More often than not it works and Lynn will tell me what's bothering her. Again, communication and actually listening to your partners concerns is a real help.

Another method you can try is 'Brain Dump'; write down on a piece of paper what is causing the anger. Once you have finished off loading your brain, take the piece of paper, tear it up, screw it up and throw it in the bin so it's gone from your mind. This method is particularly effective at night when thoughts are spinning around inside your mind and keeping you awake. We both find this is effective in not just dealing with anger but anything that is on your mind keeping you awake. Dealing with anger is about identifying what is causing it, if it's something completely obvious you have done completely unrelated to fibro then sorry just take it and deal with it!

More often than not it's fibro that causes the anger so don't automatically assume it is you and react in a negative way to it. Much of the time it isn't actually anger, its frustration and anxiety at being at the subjected to what fibro has to offer.
Remember it isn't necessarily you, its fibro.

Frustration.

"Promise me you'll always remember: You're braver than you believe, and stronger than you seem, and smarter than you think" – A. A. Milne

Frustration affects everyone involved with fibro, not only the fibro sufferer but also the caring partners. Why? it's the constant feeling of being powerless to make your partner better, to nurse them back to full health. For me, it is the confusion of not knowing why I can't make it all better. The frustration of seeing the person I love and care about in constant pain, which is ever present, just varying in intensity. Watching the fatigued look on her face as she is so tired, she can't even think straight.

Frustration affects the sufferer, the feeling of letting their loved ones down. Not being able to do the things they once did, the loss of their career, the simple fun things with family and friends. The frustration that at this moment in time there is no cure so they are stuck with it and for the foreseeable future, life is not going to be fibro free.

Frustration can be greatly lessened with understanding and empathy. Understanding what the symptoms of fibro are and the effects they have so that you don't get frustrated with your partner when they get words mixed up, drift off mid conversation or get distracted when you are trying to tell them something. Try to understand why your partner suddenly doesn't feel up to going to a social event that you have been looking forward to.

The list of effects is long and it is a matter of making the effort to understand. Reassure your partner that it doesn't matter if a social engagement has to be cancelled at short notice, suggest a relaxing night in instead.
Don't criticize, it really doesn't help either of you and just ends up causing more stress and frustration and creates a vicious circle where nobody is happy.

What helps is empathy:

Imagine for a moment, in fact, close your eyes and imagine this: It's you who has had to give up a career you enjoyed. It's you that can't do the fun things you used to do. It's you who hurts like hell and can't play ball with the kids. It's you who has very little libido, not interested in some bedroom action and your partner thinks you have gone off them or accuses you of having an affair because you aren't interested in the romantic side of your relationship.
One day you are able to walk for a few miles, the next day you can hardly walk around the house, because of the pain.

All these things cause frustration and when you get asked questions like; "But you managed okay yesterday, why not today, what's your problem?" The frustration increases and symptoms worsen the vicious circle. The point I am trying hopefully to make here is, put yourself in your partner's position and ask yourself: "If it was me, what would I want from my partner?"

Guilt.

"Do not believe the things you tell yourself when you're sad and alone."

Guilt is a common emotion with fibro sufferers.

> A person with fibro can feel guilty for not being able to do as many of the, fun activities they used to with you, the kids and family or friends any more. Guilty for letting you and others down at the last minute for social events because of a sudden fibro attack. Guilty at not being able to contribute to society as much or the family income if, like my partner they have had to give up working, especially when it was a job they enjoyed. Guilty because they have to be at home but can't keep up with the household chores as they would like to or as they think you would expect. Guilty for not being the person they used to be and not being able to do things they used to.

Some even blame themselves for getting fibro!!

Remember; No matter how bad fibro affects you or makes you feel your partner will probably be feeling a whole lot worse.

I have lost count of the number of times I used to catch Lynn crying when she thought she was out of sight alone.

How can we help?

Don't point the finger!!

Nobody is at fault for having fibro. Nobody is to blame. The one with fibro can often feel guilty for having it. Silly thoughts go through the mind "What did I do wrong?" I'm sorry I can't go to the party tonight I hate letting you down" and many other similar thoughts.

Never blame the person for having it, don't look for reasons to blame, for example: "well if you hadn't done that you wouldn't have got it", "it's your own fault for not looking after yourself better"

Remember, the person who has fibro is not at fault for having it, so don't point the finger of blame, it really doesn't help.

Accept that fibro is a life changing condition, that there will be good days and bad days. The more support and understanding your partner get, the more good days there will be, the ball is in your court.

Adjust your expectations. Sit down together and talk about what your expectations are, what you would like to do? Yes, I know, 'everything you used to' is the obvious answer to that one. Reality Check!! You can't, sorry to be blunt but it's the truth.

What you can do is make a realistic list of what you would like to achieve on good days and what you need to do to achieve them.

For example: It maybe you want to go to the coast for a day out, in our case we would make sure Lynn had a restful day the day before, plan things (as covered in the paragraph on 'Travel' in the chapter on 'Pain')

Help your partner 'Reframe.' Reframing is changing the way we 'self- talk' An example of self-talk is, your partner needing a rest in the day and telling themselves, "I am so lazy for wanting to rest in the middle of the day."
Reframing that is changing it to something like "I need to rest now so I have energy for when the kids are home from school"

Get the idea?

A don't moment!! Don't say something like "wish I could have a nap in the day when I don't want to do any work!!"

DO say something like "you can't help being tired, if you need to rest then rest, you will feel better for it, if you push yourself now you will feel worse, so go and rest"

Lynn is a naturally active person. She doesn't want to be tired in the day; she wants to be out doing things, taking action, what she doesn't need is to be criticized for how she feels.

Help your partner accept that they need to 'pace 'themselves and not push on regardless until they collapse in a painful heap.

Another thing Lynn used to feel guilty about was what she perceived to be always 'moaning' to me about being tired or hurting or feeling depressed. Reframe this by assuring your partner, "you are not moaning, you are letting me know how you feel, I need to know so I know what we are dealing with today and how I can help"

These are just a couple of examples of Reframing.

Reframing is basically identifying the negative and unhelpful thoughts and adapting them into positive helpful thoughts.

Shifting Attention

When your partner is feeling guilty about whatever it is that's bothering them at that particular time, being tired in the day, cancelling social engagements at the last minute, whatever it may be, one way of shifting attention is asking the question "is feeling this way making you feel better or worse, is it productive?"

Re-assure them that whatever it is that is causing the guilt isn't their fault, its fibro.

Another alternative is shifting the attention completely, talk about something you both enjoy, with Lynn I talk about the horses or holidays. Think of something positive or productive your partner has done recently and focus their mind on that. With Lynn it's doing something that has benefited the kids or the horses.

Remember: One of the major causes of fibro-flares is Emotional Stress, the best way to reduce emotional stress is to understand what fibro is, what effect it has and support your partner.

For a fibro sufferer, the emotional relief of being understood and supported makes a huge difference. The more understanding and support your partner have, the fewer the bad days, the fewer the bad days the more fun days you both have.

It's not rocket science people; it just takes a little effort.

Depression.

"Sometimes you will be in control of your illness and other times you'll sink into despair, and that's OK! Freak out, forgive yourself, and try again tomorrow." — Kelly Hemingway

Depression is, I think one of if not the most difficult to deal with, not only as a partner but for the person who has fibro. Depression can be caused by many things in everyday life but for someone with fibromyalgia it is part and parcel of the condition.

According to research, depression is caused by chemical imbalances in the brain, fibromyalgia is a chemical imbalance in the brain and when things aren't balanced depression sets in. Again I'm not going to start quoting research and medical terminology, this information is readily available on the Internet or indeed on some of the support group pages.

Over 75% of relationships involving Chronic Conditions end in separation/divorce. I personally think depression plays a major part in this it can be extremely difficult to deal with. I read about partners who have walked out because they can't deal with the mood swings and depression. Personally, I have not experienced the desire to walk away, in fact the opposite, it is my partner Lynn who has thought more about ending our relationship as she felt it wasn't fair on me or I suddenly started getting on her nerves.

Depression is something that can cause either partner to express a desire to walk away from the other or indeed just to get away from everything. Depression can create so much self-doubt which is damaging. Dealing with it requires some strength of character to know it isn't you its fibro. Depression has such a noticeable effect as it hits without warning, one minute everything is sunshine and smiles then literally overnight everything can change, triggered by who knows what? One day you are wanted, your company is a pleasure the next you feel as if you are being pushed away, discarded, the qualities you have that your partner normally finds endearing and attractive are suddenly an annoyance, one night your partner is wanting you to cuddle and hold them all nice and warm in bed, the next they don't even want you in the house or anywhere near them.

Depression can be brought on by various things individually or a combination of things such as, pain, fatigue, frustration caused by cognitive dysfunction (fibro fog) or your partner is just overwhelmed by demands made by family, house & garden chores that they want to do but their body won't allow. This is where communication plays a big part, talk about it, if only briefly, ask what the cause is and discuss (if your partner wants to) what can be done to combat the depression. Sometimes the best thing to do is just give your partner space and time to deal with it their own way. Sometimes being too caring can have the opposite effect of what you are trying to accomplish.

Understanding and supporting your partner on a daily basis and reducing the effects of the symptoms of fibro does in our experience greatly reduce the frequency of bouts of depression. The frequency of Lynn's depression is minimal compared to a few years ago and this we both believe is due to understanding, support and communication.

Dealing with depression does take a degree of self-confidence and strength of character and also confidence in your partners love for you.

Remember if you are a supportive understanding partner on a daily basis then you can be assured when depression does come to visit:

Remember: It's not you, its fibro.

Part Two

Fibro - Lynn's Story

My name is Lynn, I have fibromyalgia.

I am fortunate enough to have a partner who fully understands what I go through on a daily basis and supports me in any way he can.

My partners name is Pete, the author of this book.

The reasons I am contributing to this book are:

Firstly, I want to support Pete in his efforts to raise awareness of fibromyalgia and how important support is in combatting it. Secondly, to show how having the support needed can make such a huge difference to how someone with fibro copes, the significant difference to quality of life, support and understanding provide.

Support is so important but what is equally important is my attitude to fibro, I will not let it beat me.

To combat fibro I firmly believe that you have to be willing to try new things, experiment to establish what works and what doesn't even if it involves a bit more suffering when something doesn't work. We have spent years trying new regimes, products, making changes to daily routines, adapting to new challenges to live the best life possible not just as a couple but for me personally. I now live a far more productive and enjoyable life with fibro than I used to.

Unhelpful Behaviour V's Supportive Relationship

I'm not going to go into the story of how I think fibromyalgia developed for me, I'm going to start from when I got diagnosed.

I was employed as a Project Management Consultant, a very high powered and demanding job which I loved. It was a highly paid job which afforded me a fantastic lifestyle, with nice cars, travel and no financial worries.

I fell pregnant and my pregnancy was a difficult one resulting in a traumatic delivery with numerous follow up surgeries and treatments needed. As soon as I could I returned to work as I was the main income provider and my then husband stayed home to look after our son.

As time went on my aches and pains increased in frequency and worsened. I felt fatigue like I had never felt before. My cognitive ability deteriorated. The job I did previously with no trouble became increasingly difficult. As I physically and mentally deteriorated so did my relationship with my husband.

Eventually after numerous examinations and tests, I was diagnosed with this thing called fibromyalgia!

As time went on and my symptoms worsened, I had to give up my career; I simply could not manage it any longer. This caused problems in our marriage, every relationship is different, ours was not the best by any means before fibromyalgia joined us, so with it and the fact my husband could not understand or accept it and things went from bad to worse.

Accepting the diagnosis:

For me it was a grieving process of the career I had to give up, the lifestyle I would no longer be able to have and the financial security it provided. For my husband it was a grieving process of me no longer being the woman he married. I was no longer the successful businesswoman with a fantastic income that he married. Fibro meant our life would have to change; we would have to adapt to overcome. My husband would now have to be the main provider. The changes inevitably caused friction between us; he could not accept the changes and our relationship deteriorated. We went to numerous counselling sessions to help us communicate but he could not accept my condition and the distance between us became greater, ending in divorce.

Never, ever underestimate how tiring one argument can be. When one is followed by another, then another until they are a constant feature in your relationship then your stress levels and fibro flares will be more regular and severe.

Communication is the key. There were times in the early days of our relationship Pete struggled to understand what was happening with me but then it was up to me to take the time and find the energy to answer his questions and explain my feelings, what was happening to my body my brain and why I behaved in certain ways sometimes. Yes, it was tiring but it's necessary if you want support. Pete soon learned that all he needed was a direction to go in and all I needed to do was give him a brief insight, he would listen to what I had to say, then go and do his own research, to increase his knowledge and understanding of my condition.

Acceptance of the condition is the first and most important and most difficult step that both need to take, neither of you like the diagnosis, neither want it but it has happened, the only way to move on is by accepting it.

Since then I have without doubt learned the difference between unhelpful behaviour and helpful behaviour.

Helpful supportive behavior did eventually come with knowledge, time, divorce and now a partner who cares enough to spend time and even money undergoing training courses in Coaching and other helpful learning to help understand what fibro means to our lives.

Pete continues to learn, even with the amount of knowledge he has gained, he always wants to learn more.

Unhelpful Behavior:

For me, what hurt most and caused me the most stress and upset was the repetitive 'picking' at me. Hurtful comments were common: "you're too sensitive," "get over it", "stop complaining", "you're lazy" and "you're over-reacting". These kinds of comments did nothing but result in stress headaches and physical pain in my joints.

If I cried it was a release of the pain it took me a long time to realise this as I'm not a crying kinda girl and when I did break down and cry, the cruel verbal taunts would continue.

I did develop a method of coping with the insults and taunts by thinking how to turn the comments round in my head, what I now know as 'reframing'

If I take each negative comment from above and turn it around, hopefully you will see where I am coming from on this.

Negative Comments

"You're too sensitive":
Yes, I am too sensitive, especially physically - fibro causes Hyper sensitivity to all elements, such as touch, taste and smell.
A hyper sensitivity to things audible and visual, at times over sensitivity to peoples' comments.

"Get over it"

How I wish I could, just like I would get over a cold! This is a comment he would make because he didn't know and didn't want to know how to deal with fibro, what he could do to help and support me. If I asked for help or an input on how to manage fibro the standard answer would be "You'll just have to get over it" i can't 'get over' fibro but I
can get over his issues and insecurities about fibro by gaining knowledge about managing fibro myself.
fibro isn't going anywhere. It can however be managed.

"Stop complaining"

I have found that if I vocalise how I feel then it's done, that's it, I move on to how to feel better. When I apologise

to Pete for moaning he tells me I'm not moaning just letting him know how I feel. That way he knows he's not done anything wrong to cause me to be quiet.
"You're lazy"

If I don't rest when I need rest then I'll only feel worse. I'm not being lazy, I'm just looking after myself. It's hard enough for me to stop, so accepting rest will prevent a flare is tough, especially when I'm on a roll. 'Pacing'
The official fibro description and is one of the hardest things to master. Pete is actually more in tune with my energies than me, he spots when I'm struggling long before I'll admit it and will deflect me from what I'm doing by asking simple questions like, "shall we have a break for a bit" or "is it time for a cuppa" suggestions that cause me to just stop for a while.

"You're over-reacting"

Fibro is a central sensitivity syndrome. It isn't me that is over reacting it's my body that is. The reason I feel the way I do is because my body is a 'Drama Queen' it feels like I'm on the starting line for the 100 metres sprint and that's when I'm lying in bed!
At times I will lie in bed and try to talk myself into relaxing, my neck and shoulders are solid with pain or at least that's what it feels like to me. Pete is now the master 'de-knotting' my back! The muscles tense and knot up, a nice massage using magnesium oil helps a great deal.

Helpful Supportive Behaviour

Helpful supportive behaviour did eventually come with knowledge, time, divorce and now a partner who cares enough to have spent time to learn about my condition and how he can support me. Pete even spent a lot of money undergoing a training course in Coaching to help understand what fibro means to our lives and how he can support me. Pete continues to learn, even with the amount of knowledge he has gained, he always wants to learn more.
Supportive behaviour not only comes in the form of physical help, being there for me when I need help but also comes in the form of knowing when to leave me alone.

A very important note I want to add in here is - quite often I need space, not only physical but mental space. What's in my head is often overwhelming as I fail to reason the what and why of what's happening to my mind and body. This must be very tough for Pete and the rest of my family. It's not personal to them its more a necessity for my sanity at times.

Physically, my whole family know that if I've disappeared, I've gone off for a 'power nap' or to listen to a relaxation CD they all respect that I need it to function. Mentally the family also know sleep narcosis can be a major factor, (sometimes Amitriptylene knocks me out until late morning of the following day) so until 11am they don't ask me any questions because they won't get a comprehensible answer! On these days I 'potter' around the house doing tasks that take no thinking about. I have a list on my iPad so I don't even need to think what to do. (I just have to remember to check my I pad!)

Sometimes I need time and space to work out the 'Best way forward, 'Do Just One Thing' and don't be too hard on myself. To have a partner that understands my needs and has confidence in themselves to handle the request is worth its weight in gold. Support and understanding are so important and it is great to have someone who supports me in everything I try but as the one who has fibromyalgia, what I am prepared to do for myself is even more important.

What I am trying to convey is that it is up to you to take responsibility for your condition and your new life. I only wish I'd of spent less time pretending it didn't exist which resulted in the 'boom and bust' scenario. It is up to you how you face fibro, only you can take action in dealing with it. Yes, it is fantastic to have support and it does make a massive difference but the ultimate responsibility is yours.

I hate to say it but 'pacing' is the lesson to be learnt and if you are someone like me who used to have a fast-paced demanding but enjoyable career it is one of the most difficult new regimes to adapt to.
There are numerous counselling/support services within the health systems around the world but for me there is no substitute for experience when being the partner of anyone with any Chronic Condition not just fibro.

Pete after sixteen years of knowing me, eleven years of being my partner, together with his own studies, now has that experience and knowledge to share.

What I would also say to people with fibro, is don't be afraid to try new things, to try just one thing today that may benefit you. Everyone is different, some things work for one and not for another, I know how frustrating it can be to try something that doesn't benefit you. I have tried and tested so many products, over the years, many of which gave me little or no relief from my symptoms but I now have a catalogue of items and coping strategies that work for me. Don't be afraid to try different things to see which work for you.

I hear what you are saying that this can run into a lot of money, we have spent a lot of money over the years searching for helpful products that actually work. I am happy to say the things that work best have been the low-cost items, so don't be fooled into thinking you have to spend a fortune to find some relief.

Finding new ways to understand your partner and help each other remain positive can be fun.
Firstly; anything that isn't negative is positive, so try to refrain from negative thoughts, words or actions. It is now your chance to rediscover and re-invent your relationship if you wish. Your life together has changed with the introduction of fibromyalgia into your relationship.

There is presently no cure, so if you want your relationship to flourish and not fall apart you have to accept and adapt. The person you fell in love with is still there but now they have a burden to carry, the burden that it's, it is a heavy burden, too heavy to carry alone. It will take its toll on both of you, it will cause both of you to react in ways that will be alien to each other, both of you will see changes in behavior in each other, not just the person who has the condition. As a couple you form a loving bond, you understand each other, fibromyalgia changes things, now you have to find new ways of understanding each other.

Pete's comments:

Lynn's story is tragic and whilst the causes of how she came to have Fibromyalgia may be unique to her, the story isn't. I am in no doubt that there are thousands if not millions of others who have experienced a similar story of how fibro has affected their lives. What I find inspirational about Lynn is her never say die attitude, her willingness to keep on trying, if something works use it, if it doesn't move on and try something else. Lynn doesn't dwell on the things she can't do, she focuses and enjoys the things she can do and is always willing to try. To me, Lynn is an exceptional woman who will not be beaten.

"You shouldn't focus on why you can't do something, which is what most people do. You should focus on why perhaps you can, and be one of the exceptions." – Steve Case

Accounts from others with fibromyalgia.

Some time ago I did some research on how fibro affects other people, the following pages are in response to the questions I asked people. The people in the following pages are all from different places in the world, different ages, different backgrounds but they all have one thing in common, their lives have been changed by fibromyalgia.

Kirsty's story:

I'm 27 now and had the car crash at 19. By the age of 23 I reduced my hours from 39.5 to 35 per week , this gave me respite on Wednesday afternoons to give me some form of energy to finish Thursday and Friday, although I would spend the majority of the weekend in bed and then the whole cycle begin again on Monday morning. By 24 I resigned and am now doing 24 hours a week, a whole 15.5 hours less than when I worked full time.
The things that affect me most are: aching/pain, tiredness, stiffness especially in morning and late evenings.
I have gone from full time work to part time which has helped reduce the extreme pain and exhaustion. My boss allows me to start at 10am instead of 9am to avoid sitting in rush hour traffic, I also finish work before rush hour in the evening either at 3pm or 4pm depending on which day it is. If I drive for too long or have to sit in traffic I get flare ups. I have aches and pains everyday but with the hours and diet I do its bearable. On a semi bad day I will take paracetamol and rest as much as I can (I try not to take

tablets, if I did every time you would hear me rattling!) I have found reflexology helps and after having it regularly for 6 years I have worked up to a gap of 8 weeks between treatment. I started with 2 treatments a week. I take vitamins and try to eat lots of veg, fruit and I find protein helps too. If I eat too many carbs or junk food I usually end up with a flare up.

I try to go for a walk once a week but this is not always possible. Last year I got up to walking/ exercising 2 to 3 times a week but since September my body has not allowed this.

My partner is my best support system.

He helps with cleaning of the house as I find this at times excruciating in my upper body and wrists.

He also does the cooking as I find after a day's work this is really hard and if I do I end up flaring up and setting myself up for an exhausting day for the next day

He encourages me to rest and will do pressure points on my feet in between reflexology treatments which I have picked up and taught him over the last 6 years of receiving treatment.

What happens when I'm on a really bad day?

On a really bad day bed rest and the strongest co- codamol "numbs" the pain but I tend to feel quite sick because of the tablets so it's a vicious circle.

Kirsty

Debbie's story:

Hi there, so glad to hear that fibro is being looked at and studied more ♣ I'm Debbie, 46 & a sufferer of fibro. I was told it was brought on by my previous condition of DDD.(disk degeneration disease). I have also been diagnosed with breast cancer at the age of 39and still focusing on getting to remission. Knowing what I know now, I have suffered with fibro for many years before actually getting diagnosed.

The way I describe my symptoms... My sleep is very irrational, sometimes days without any. My body feels like lead on days, & the mornings I feel highly 'hung over')? It takes my meds
(tramadol) about hour to take effect. I get muscle ache/ bone ache spasmodic pulses which drive me insane. I feel constantly flu like. As for brain fog, it scares me!! I totally know what I'm thinking & want to say, but my memory goes blank. I get so frustrated. My mobility is chronically affected by my other conditions, but the fibro, will just totally stop my mechanics from wanting to work. It makes me feel as though I'm being lazy? But physically I am unable to do it. I feel the cold massively, it make me sore & clumsy& agitated. Warmth helps. Tens machine makes me worse. Moods are a battle. Feeling of being nervy inside of my body drives me mad. Hopes this helps need more support & understanding
Good luck ☺
Debbie.

Carol's story:

My name is Carol and I would like to express my 3 things I find mostly unbearable
I have had this condition 22 years now and the first thing Would be the stiffness and pain throughout my body the second thing is the swelling of my hands causing pain and weakness and difficult to use the third thing is extreme tiredness so bad its hard to think how I cope with the day let alone working as well. My GP has given me bu trans patches for my pain plus amitriptyline I would love to know if there was more to help me.
Regards
Carol

Steve's story:

Hi,
My name is Steve
Pain management and Fibro fog for me are the worst. I have recently returned to work and find that the management have no understanding, there is very little in the way of awareness in the work place for this condition. We all know that Fibromyalgia needs better understanding from a medical point of view also more needs to be done for the sufferer's mental wellbeing too. We are all filled with very harmful depressing drugs that seem to do very little for us except lead us down a steep, fast road to depression.

Thank you for all you are doing.

20 Useful tips to help each other

The following pages contain a list of tips and quotes which may help to remain positive and not fall under the black cloud of negative thoughts/energy. They are written from Lynn's perspective as the person with fibro and mine as the partner.

1. Believe your partner: listen to and hear what they say. Feelings of intimacy and closeness can pull a relationship through hard times and help couples thrive when the relationship is good.
One way to build intimacy in your relationship is by sharing your thoughts and feelings with each other and then responding to those disclosures in a way that makes you both feel good.
Being a responsive partner, and feeling like your partner is responsive to you, is really at the core of good communication and closeness. When you feel like your partner really gets you, you feel like nothing else matters.
"Your circumstance doesn't make life extraordinary. Love Does" – Trina Harmon

2. Enjoy the little things in life every day.

"Enjoy the little things, for one day you may look back and realise they were the big things." – Robert Brault

Spend time in nature, enjoy the beauty that surrounds you, appreciate it and enjoy its calming influence, take walks (even short ones) or just sitting in a favourite place together will help keep the closeness in your relationship.

Meditation, this is something both Lynn and I have found a great help, find a method that works for you and you are comfortable with. Yoga works for some, for me it doesn't, I find it uncomfortable, my chosen method is mindfulness, which is something I can do anywhere any time.

Prayer. For the religious among you, prayer offers great comfort.

Spend time with children/grandchildren, nieces /nephews, as they know how to live in the moment. Children are a great tonic, they don't look too far ahead they just enjoy the moment, they can teach us all about coping by just following their lead and enjoying the moment.

3. Don't sweat the small stuff, enjoy laughter.

"With the fearful strain that is on me night and day, if I did not laugh I should die" – Abraham Lincoln

These are very appropriate words for all those whose life is affected by fibromyalgia.

Laughter triggers the release of endorphins, the body's natural feel good chemicals. Endorphins promote an overall sense of well-being and can even temporarily relieve pain, in my experience.

Don't get anxious about the little things that crop up. For example. The Situation: Your husband is running late (not his fault) to look after the little one while you go to an appointment, you're going to be late for your appointment and your toddler is wiping messy hands on your skirt, stay calm and problem solve. A late spouse and a messed-up skirt aren't catastrophes

Stop and think "How am I going to solve this?" Once you phrase the question in your mind, you have awakened the reasoning portion of your brain and put yourself in a position to find an answer. No longer are you a victim of your emotions.

The next step is to pretend you are a coach with a game plan, such as pulling on a clean skirt, taking your child with you, and texting your husband to meet you at your appointment.

So, don't sweat it just take the action necessary to resolve it.

4. Don't try to change your partner, accept them for who they now are.

Don't try and fight it, to succeed in your battle with fibro you will need to adapt.

"Every success story is a tale of constant adaption, revision and change." – Richard Branson.

The thing we all have to accept as partners is, no matter what we do, we cannot change the fact our loved one has fibromyalgia; we can't buy a bottle of magic pills to make it go away.

What we can do is accept it and try to understand it. We can work with our partner to find ways of improving the situation.

Communicate with each other if something works, stick with it, if it doesn't revise what you are doing and change it.

5. Stay in the now, not the past, focus on the positives.

"Do not dwell in the past, do not dream of the future, concentrate the mind on the present moment" – Buddha

By this I mean that my awareness is completely focused on the here and now. The past, the future – they don't exist, take things one day at a time.

Have your focus, your attention, your thoughts and feelings all fixed on the task at hand.

Minimise what you let into your head early in the day. Email, Facebook, online Websites, Twitter, I found that I hade so many thoughts bouncing around in my head.

What this means to me is that it becomes harder and harder to concentrate on anything, to stay in the now and not to be dragged away into some negative thought loop.

My solution is to minimize these things then my day becomes lighter and simpler and I not only stay in the now more easily but I also tend to get more things of importance done.

6. Help them remember they always have a choice.

"The joy we feel has little to do with the circumstances of our lives and more to do with the focus of our lives" – Russell M Nelson

You may have looked at your circumstances and thought you were going through this because you "don't have a choice"?
True, you didn't choose to have fibromyalgia but you do have a choice how you live with it.
How many people do you hear say "I have no other option", "I need to do this", "I have to do this, that and the other?" You are not alone! If this myth were actually true, there would be no self-help industry?! Is it hopeless to think we can actually make the changes we want to make? No, it isn't hopeless at all. But it isn't going to happen just like that!

"You always have two choices: your commitment versus your fear" - Sammy Davis Junior

7. Don't be afraid to ask questions.

He who asks question remains a fool for 5 minutes. He who does not ask, remains a fool forever." Ancient Chinese proverb

Remember – the internet isn't always right. Nowadays it's easy to circulate unverified information. Whilst there is a huge amount of good information out there it can also be a huge challenge to filter the good info from the bad. This is where finding a trusted human element is really important. Reach out and find respected educators or professionals can be a great way to find the answers you are looking for in relation to dealing with issues of fibromyalgia symptoms, fibromyalgia pain and the many other issues this condition raises.

8. Do something each day that you want to do.

"Every day is a new day, and you'll never be able to find happiness if you don't move on". – Carrie Underwood

Take some action planning Steps such as:
Chose something YOU want to do. Make it Achievable.
Be action-specific, decide what do you have to do in order to achieve it?
Answer these questions:
What and how much?
What is your confidence level? Score it out of 10, if it's a 7 or more? then just do it if it's less than a 7 think just how much you want to do it?
Start off with the small things, success in lots of little things can make you happier than not achieving one big thing.

9. Don't act like everything is fine all the time.

"You think everything's OK, and it is – 'till it's not." – Ani Difranco

Some people wear their smile like a disguise their eyes will tell the truth, if they sparkle, they are in good shape, if they are dull and lifeless, something is not right.

I see myself as an optimistic person but even the most optimistic of people have days (or weeks, or months) when they can't see the bright side of a dark situation. This is tough especially when you're used to pulling up your big girl pants, pushing forward and refusing to be beaten by anything.

When this happens, I feel defeated and hopeless, even if it's only temporary, even if the situation is understandable, it can still make everything up to that point feel like it has been a waste of my time.

So what do I do?
I allow myself to feel bad or sad for a while without feeling guilty and it passes, the bad feelings compound if you feel guilty about it.

Realise that you can't fix everything, real optimism isn't about magically making a bad situation sunny, it's about finding the rays of light even in the worst of situations.

10. Remember, it's okay to fall apart sometimes. Give yourself and your partner permission to do so.

"Never be afraid to fall apart because it is an opportunity to rebuild you the way you wish you had been all along". – Rae Smith

11. Feel the misery, you may shout, cry, throw a tantrum, whatever needs to be done to get over that first wave of pain.
 Deep breaths can help to settle the mind, body and soul, four breaths in and four out.
Don't try and do everything alone. A supportive friend/partner will work wonders.
Especially when I attempt to use messenger, WhatsApp, iPhone or SKYPE to speak to my friend
laughing all the way through the bad connections.
Confiding in a friend works wonders, my friend listens to my woes, empathizes with me then empowers me to get moving or at the very least change my state.
Reschedule and slow it down, unplug from the net, let your voicemail get it, anything and I mean anything that can wait until tomorrow, leave it till tomorrow. Take care of you first.
Take one step and then another and another. Your new world won't be built in a day. Make it through the next 10 mins is another option here.
"It'll Pass" which is my own personal saying.

12. Help them accept change is part of life and doesn't have to be a disaster.

"Your life does not get better by chance, it gets better by change." – Jim Rohn

It's not about the changes, it is about how we react to these changes, accept the changes and understand change is for a reason.
Not everything that is faced can be changed; but remember that nothing can be changed until it is actually faced.
My personal favourite, the more responsibility you take the more successful your life will be.

Help to practice emotional awareness, can you identify what you are feeling and why, no matter what it is.

It's tough sometimes to recognize one's own emotions. People who can do this successfully are able to identify the subtle differences in their emotions and know how their emotions affect their behaviour, decisions and performance. Lesser mortals such as myself have the conflict of pain causing emotions to battle with rational. If you are unaware of what's going on inside of you, you can't influence or change it. Practice, practice, practice, the skills of emotional-self-awareness you will get the insights you need to be able to change it to your benefit. To know your "who, what when and why things push your buttons" is a strategy to take control of your situations.

How I hear you ask?

Identify when your "hot buttons" are pushed, recognize which situations or people are pushing those buttons and understand the triggers for your emotional reactions by reflecting on what you believe and value.

13. Think about one thing that is positive or good about your situation.
One of the first things I worked on once I got over the grief of my 'old life' was to work consciously with my own personal development to improve my outlook on life by figuring out what is the positive or good in a situation and what is the opportunity to learn in this situation?
It has taken me a very long time to learn to ask these two simple questions. This was because of the emotional turmoil and shock of being diagnosed with fibromyalgia.
Be careful what you let into your mind and space. Negativity from people or things can drag you down, can you think of any? Consider this for the coming week. Spend less time with one of those people or sources of negativity and how you can spend more of the time you have now freed up with one of the most positive sources or people in your life.

14. Go a little more slowly in whatever you are doing.
Don't rush things, then your mind will slow down and you will get more clarity in your thoughts.

15. Don't let a molehill become a mountain.
Say stop, breathe and re- focus on the issue and a resolution. Again, don't rush into activating a swift

resolution to a situation, stop and think for as long as it takes.

16. Value your lives.

"The ultimate value of life depends upon awareness and the power of contemplation rather than mere survival" Aristotle

Again, it's down to choice, you can choose to merely survive through your life with fibro or you can contemplate how to make the best of it.

17. Learn to take criticism in a healthy, positive way
Don't react or reply immediately, soak it up, evaluate it and remember criticism isn't always directed at or about you. Help each other, trust in each other to let out whatever feelings you have, listening speaks volumes, listen twice as much as you speak, its why we have 2 ears and 1 mouth? Instead of looking for something interesting to say, be interested. Trust that asking and listening is enough
When it comes to talking with someone about their difficult time, what is needed most is for you to be quiet and listen, avoid giving advice and hold back on that compulsion to give perspective and tell someone how to think or feel, for example: "you need to buck up, things happen for a reason"
Finally and most importantly avoid making comparisons to your own or other people's experiences

18. Start the day in a positive way.
Give yourself at least 15 minutes of no screen time. Swap the coffee for a glass of hot lemon. Sit up correctly ready to face the day. Set out your day how you want it to be. Establish your goal. Maybe do some gentle stretches. Meditate for a while or do breathing exercises Appreciate the little things that will be part of your day
Say thank you to yourself for being positive

19. Help separate fact from fiction.
Your life is reality; learn how to stop negative thoughts because that is all they are, thoughts.
When something is bothering you, you know that getting it off your mind is easier said than done, If you tell yourself not to think about something then that's all you're going to think about! which is unpleasant and counterproductive and, in some cases, lead to chronic depression.
If you are having trouble getting something 'out of your head' write it all out on a piece of paper and throw it away, physically throw it away! or If I have a problem, I can't solve then I write a letter to my subconscious and ask it to answer the question? Try it, write it out and put it under your pillow, next morning take the paper, read it and 'ping' the answer will pop out of your brain.
Find comfort in warming up with a cup of tea (or whatever your favourite hot drink is). If you are focused on feeling lonely try to substitute physical warmth for emotional warmth, it can be a quick fix.

20. Never forget that you are unique

"Let your hope, not your hurts, shape your future" – Robert Schuller

As a person with fibromyalgia or as the partner of someone with fibromyalgia, you are unique, how you use your uniqueness is your choice. You can submit to fibro or look for the chinks in its armour that let your happy days shine through.

"Never forget that if there weren't any need for you in all your uniqueness to be on this earth, you wouldn't be here in the first place. And never forget, no matter how overwhelming life's challenges and problems seem to be, that one person can make a difference in the world. In fact, it is always because of one person that all the changes that matter in the world come about. So be that one person" – R. Buckminister Fuller

Caring for your partner

In this book we have looked at how important it is for a partner to understand and support the person who has fibro but what about the partner?

Your condition can also be hard on your partner and for them to remain supportive and helpful they may also need some support from you, not physically but emotionally. Lynn and I work together; we help each other in different ways.

It's easy to fall into the trap of believing the only person who needs help is the person with fibro but that is simply not true, it is something you have to face together and helping each other gives both a sense of purpose.

This chapter covers some of the ways that have worked for us to help ease the stress placed on the caregiver.

Don't fake being well, don't put on a happy face when you feel like hell, it doesn't help your partner understand what's going on. You need to be honest about how you are feeling and your limitations for the day. If you are not honest about this it can confuse your partner and ultimately lead to a feeling of guilt for not recognizing how bad you feel.
For example: you put on your happy face and so your partner becomes enthusiastic about an activity which you then embark on, believing you are up to it. The activity results in chronic pain that could have been avoided by being honest in the first place, the partner then feels really bad about suggesting it and refrains from suggesting things in the future for fear of placing a burden on you.

Yes, I know in a previous chapter we talked about recognizing signs of it being a good day or bad day by looking at body language but we all make mistakes, your confirmation of how you are feeling is the only 100% sure way. Be honest about your limitations, frustrations and pain. Only by being open with each other you work out a plan to deal with them and enjoy the best of each other

Be sure your caregiver is taking care of his or her own health.

There's a tendency for partners to ignore any medical symptoms that they might develop that aren't as severe as yours are. Something I will openly admit I am guilty of. As a result, you may have to push your partner to seek medical help. And if your partner is being treated for something, even if it's minor, don't forget to ask how he or she is doing!

Discuss with your partner what you need them to do for you, what you can or can't do. If you don't your partner is likely to think that they have to do everything. This can lead to burnout and can also compromise your partner's health. It can also frustrate the hell out of you by your partner taking on the 'Mother Hen' role and fussing too much.

Once you have established what you need help with, look at utilising other services and family members/friends who are willing to help by asking them to do certain things. For example, use online shopping, unless of course shopping is something you enjoy doing together.

Whilst there are regular tasks that are necessary that you and your partner don't enjoy, another family member may not mind and even enjoy doing, such as cleaning. Yep I said it; some people I know actually enjoy cleaning.

Remember if you can save energy by delegating the tasks you don't enjoy, it conserves energy to do things you do enjoy.

Many people are taught or have the belief that it is weak to ask for help, it isn't. When I have been asked for help, I have never thought of that person as weak, I have taken it as a compliment they thought enough of me to ask. Your family/friends may be glad you asked. Sometimes people don't like to offer for fear of offending you. It's easy to assume that if someone wanted to help they would have offered, this isn't always the case, they do want to help but just need to be asked.

Find ways to preserve the relationship you had before.

Think about what made your relationship work. What makes you laugh together, okay you may not be able to cope with sitting through a comedy club night but you can watch them on TV or go to the comedy club with the knowledge that you can leave at any time.

If you enjoy cards or board games that are something you can do when you need to spend time in your bed or if you are bed bound.

You may enjoy talking about certain subjects, at times when you have the energy for conversation, sit and chat. Whatever it is that you have always enjoyed doing together try and do the same but adjust the time spent to what you can cope with. Lynn and I found by taking small baby steps to start with, our enjoyment time doing that activity has increased over time. It may well take a lot of planning and flexibility with timing etc. but it will be time well spent.

Encourage your partner to do things without you.

Partners are often reluctant to do enjoyable things for themselves. It may stem from a sense of guilt, doing something you can't or used to be able to do but no longer can. It is easy for a partner to think that they must make a 100% commitment to looking after you to not fail you, this is simply not true, it is your partner expecting too much of themselves. This is something that I personally can fully associate with. It has taken me a long time and much encouragement from Lynn to 'do something for me'

You may need as Lynn has done, take the lead in convincing your partner how important it is for them to take some time for themselves.

Let your partner know how much they are valued.

It is easy to take support for granted, something Lynn never does, she lets me know how much my support and understanding means to her and that in turn makes me feel useful, which believe me means a lot. Fibro has a great way of making partners feel useless as we cannot treat it, nurse our loved ones to full health or take the pain away for them.

Remind your partner that things can change for the better, never give up on this and talk about any improvements that have happened, it will encourage both of you to carry on.

I remember Lynn's early days with fibro; lay in bandages on her sofa, in terrible pain in a loveless marriage to a completely unsupportive and emotionally abusive husband. The difference from then to now is amazing, once she had gone through the process of divorce, shedding what was probably one of the main causes of her 'flares', things improved. As a friend I supported her and now as her life partner I do but it isn't about what I have done to support Lynn it is what she has done for herself and together, we are a team and the improvement in our life now is significant. Things can improve, Lynn is living proof of this.

Communication is the key.

Throughout this book I stress the importance of communication, so what is communication?

Communication is: the act or process of using words, sounds, signs, or behaviors to express or exchange information or to express your ideas, thoughts and feelings to someone else. It is a two-way process of reaching mutual understanding to exchange information, news, ideas and feelings to create and share meaning

Why communication is important in our lives?

It is no doubt that communication plays a vital role in human life. It not only helps to facilitate the process of sharing information and knowledge, but also helps people to develop or maintain relationships and learn how to communicate effectively to make our lives better.

Serious illness puts both people who are ill and those around them under great stress, making good communication more difficult. Fibromyalgia brings the added burden of cognitive problems. Communication can be difficult in any relationship at times but when a chronic condition such as fibromyalgia is also part of your relationship it can be even more difficult.

To improve or make the best of communication here are some tips:

Pick a Good Time and Setting

If you have something important to discuss with a significant person in your life, try to do so time when both of you are in the right frame of mind. It should be a time when both of you can pay attention to each other and not be distracted, preferably during your best hours of the day. Choose a place that you are both comfortable and relaxed, this could be a favourite bar, pub restaurant or just simply sat in your favourite room of the house, ideally without distractions or interruptions.

Focus on One Thing at a Time and Be Specific:

Focus on one issue at a time. If you want something to change or improve, be specific in your request. For example, if it's housework don't be vague saying something like "I need help with the housework." The person being asked may wonder what you want them to do. Instead, say something like, "Can you do the laundry today?" or "Can you do the grocery shopping?"

If you are the one being asked to do something then don't hesitate to ask what is expected of you. You can ask, "What specifically would you like me to do?"

Practice Good Listening Skills

Good communication is based on each person understanding the other person's views. Understanding begins with listening, which means focusing your attention on what is being said, with the goal of understanding the speaker's point of view. Let the person speaking finish what they have to say before responding, listening works best if it is done without interruption. After the person has finished speaking, acknowledge having heard them. You might say something as simple as, "I understand." Or if you don't understand then ask them to explain a bit more.

From time to time, stop and re-cap, try not to go through the whole agenda at once, check if you have understood what the other has been saying, repeating your summary of what has been said back to them is a good way of doing this. You could say, "Let me try to summarize what I've heard and you can tell me if I've understood you."

Aim for solutions:

The aim of communicating is to find solutions, not blaming one another or finding fault. The idea is to be able to discuss problems in a constructive rather than a confrontational way. Treat each other with respect, acknowledging his or her support and effort. Avoid demeaning comments, sarcasm and blaming. Acknowledge your part in shared problems and show appreciation for the other's efforts.

Use Problem Solving:

Use problem solving to find solutions. The first step of problem solving is brainstorming, which means thinking of a variety of possible ways to solve a problem. At this stage, the goal is to generate as many ideas as possible, without evaluating them.

For example, if your problem is how to do household chores when one member of the family is ill, alternatives might include dividing up the chores differently among members of the family, hiring occasional or regular assistance, simplifying tasks (for example, having simpler meals or cleaning less frequently. Lynn and I regularly use 'brain dumping' to clear our heads of things that are concerning us or we feel need to be addressed. Brain dumping is simply writing down whatever is in your head onto a piece (or pieces) of paper. Then go through them and decide which are the most important issues that require a solution and pick out one or two to start with, discuss them and find the solution then put it into practice, once you have evaluated if it has worked or not, either move on to the next issue or if the solution hasn't worked, discuss alternative solutions.

If after these processes you cannot find a suitable solution then you might consider getting some help.

In many cases, you will be able to solve your problems yourself, but at times you may want to get help, either in understanding the causes of your problem or in finding solutions. So it may help to ask what resources are available to you. Support groups on social media are a good source of help, others may have had a similar issue to yours and found a solution you hadn't thought of. You may need to ask your Doctor or support worker. There are numerous resources to find help, don't be afraid to utilise those resources to the fullest extent.

Also, if conversations about your problems are not productive, you can consider getting professional help. A counsellor a life coach with experience of fibro can help facilitate a solution to particular problems and also help you practice good problem solving skills.

Have Regular Relationship Discussions:

Something that Lynn and I find useful is setting aside time for any discussions by having a a date night, in our case we prefer home as our date night with a nice meal, bottle of wine and nobody else in the house. If that proves difficult to arrange without other family members being around we will make it a lunch date at our favourite pub. Either way it is a relaxed atmosphere with no interruptions.

We listen to the other without being defensive and really try to put ourselves in the other's shoes and feel what it's like for them. We problem-solve together to come up with a solution for any issues.

It really does work for us.

"The more that communication is practised the easier and more effective it becomes."

Quote from a very wise man. (or not! actually it's one I came up with so hope you like it)

Communicating fibro to others.

I cannot stress enough how important communication is when managing fibro but how on earth do you explain it to children, family and friends?

Explaining fibromyalgia is very difficult to do without making it over complicated. If you've had fibro for a long time, you'll probably know all about trigger points, neurotransmitters, chemical imbalances in the brain and so on. It's easy to forget how complex it is especially to someone who has no understanding of it until you notice the glazed look in their eyes when you try and explain the complexities of it.

Fibromyalgia is a complex condition that's difficult to understand because it involves the brain and nervous system and can have an impact on virtually every part of the body.

Trying to understand this condition can be incredibly confusing which in the past has led to the belief it is a psychological condition, with the theory that it's all in the mind which is simply not true, it is a very real physical condition.

With many chronic conditions, the patients are constantly visibly ill, their condition is constant and usually visibly worsens, with fibromyalgia, a person can be incapable of doing anything one day then the next able to carry out a normal day, which can be confusing for those looking in. It doesn't mean they are well or getting better it just means they are having either a bad day or a good day and they don't know until they wake up which it's going to be, making planning work or social events with any certainty virtually impossible.

So how do you explain it to others?

This is a tough one especially if you are newly diagnosed or had it for a while but still getting your own head around it, how do you explain something you don't fully understand yourself.

Lynn's way. (Which seems to work well for both of us when explaining fibro)?

It helps to read the person you are explaining it to, is it someone who is well versed in medical terminology if so use it if not keep it simple and perhaps relate it to something they are familiar with, for example when describing the pain of a flare say something like," the pain in my body is like the intense pain of a migraine, it won't last forever and it will pass but unlike a migraine which eventually goes there is a residue of pain left in my body that is always present, it just varies from day to day in intensity"

When explaining to someone else it is believe it or not more about them than you and your condition, what you are first aiming for is an acceptance that this 'something' you have is now part of your life, their life and your life together, it isn't going to kill you but you are not going to recover from it, it is there to stay for the foreseeable future but with the understanding and support of loved ones it can be managed and the extent of how it changes your life can be minimised and your relationship enhanced despite it.

What you are communicating is that 'they' are important to you and important in your future.

Lynn conducted a little experiment in understanding and asked her mother what she knows about her fibro, after all she has seen her with it since she was first diagnosed some 16 years ago although we all believe it all started following the traumatic pregnancy and delivery of her son 19 years ago which left her body in tatters requiring numerous surgeries.

Her mother explained that she knows Lynn's body over reacts to cold and wet weather.

She knows that some days are better than others but there is always an element of pain in Lynn's days and nights.

She knows how to recognise signs that indicate what sort of a day Lynn's having, the way she walks, talks and how she holds her body.

She knows that fibro like life itself evolves and with it so the explanations and answers have to, as Lynn adapts so must those around her if they are going to help.

My Mother is a great help in navigating how best to inform people who come into my life in my local environment, coming from a farming family who believe if you are stood up and breathing you are fine! She likens explain fibro to creeping ivy, little by little the understanding will evolve and stick. The one thing she doe insist upon is that Lynn communicates with her regularly so she doesn't have to worry about her or try and second guess how Lynn is and also be straight with her about how she is feeling don't dismiss how she really feels with a "I'm fine don't worry I can manage" and then later she sees Lynn in obvious pain as a result of overdoing something.

What myself and Lynn have found helpful and effective when communicating with her teenage son (and my daughter) is to refer to fibro in the third party, for example if her son wants her to do something for him or wants help with something that is not urgent and she is just too fatigued to be of any help and needs to rest she no longer says "can it wait till later I am tired" the usual response to that was "you're always tired I need, (whatever it is he needs me to do or help with) now"

Now she says "my body needs to rest it's not up to doing anything at the minute, once it's had a reboot I'll be able to help you" She uses the word reboot as that's terminology he understands for reawakening fresh and Compos Mentos.

Lynn has explained to me before that it isn't her as a person that has fibro, it's her body that does and it's her body that dictates what she as a person can do or not do at any given time, by taking the personal association out of the equation and making it physical it puts across to him that there is a situation that is only temporary and she has a way of making it better or manageable.

Earlier in this chapter I mentioned that it helps to read the person you are talking to, what we both find extremely helpful is Nunchi (Noon Chee) eye measure, which is the ancient Korean art of subtly gauging other people's thoughts and feelings before engaging them, after all there is no point even trying to explain anything whatsoever to someone who is simply not in the right frame of mind to listen to or digest what you are saying to them.

Lynn says I am a natural master of Nunchi which has proved very beneficial in our relationship with each other and our relationship with fibro.

Useful tips:

When explaining take things steady, break things to them gently and if necessary repeatedly, eventually it will dawn on them that fibro is here to stay.

Explain it bit by bit as symptoms arise, don't overwhelm them by trying to explain everything about fibro in one long session, most of what you have explained will likely be forgotten within twenty minutes.

Authors note: Nunchi (noon chee) is something as a partner I have found invaluable and of great benefit to Lynn in that I can read what sort of a day she is having or starting without her having to explain, it is something I believe all partners would benefit from, it takes away the guess work and the need to question your partner, the last thing your partner wants when having a bad day is to be questioned about it or pressed to explain it, if a partner can read the situation without the need for question or explanation this really does help in reducing stress and managing fibro.

More information about Nunchi can be found on our website fibropartners.com.

Terminology help page.

Common terms associated with fibro and other Chronic.

Analgesic	A medication or treatment that relieves pain.
Arthritis	Literally means joint inflammation, but is often used to indicate a group of more than 100 rheumatic diseases. These diseases affect not only the joints but also other connective tissues of the body, including important supporting structures such as muscles, tendons, and ligaments, as well as the protective covering of internal organs.
Autoimmune Disease	One in which the immune system destroys or attacks the patient's own body tissue.
Cartilage	A tough, resilient tissue that covers and cushions the ends of the bones and absorbs shock.
Chronic Condition	A Chronic condition is a human health condition or disease that is persistent or otherwise long-lasting in its effects or a disease that comes with time. The term chronic is often applied when the course of the disease lasts for more than three months
Cognitive Dysfunction	(also known as brain fog) is the loss of intellectual functions such as thinking, remembering, and reasoning of sufficient severity to interfere with daily functioning. Patients with cognitive dysfunction have trouble with verbal recall, basic arithmetic, and concentration.
Collagen	The main structural protein of skin, tendon, bone cartilage, and connective tissues.
Connective Tissue	The supporting framework of the body and its internal organs.

Fibromyalgia	Sometimes called fibrositis, a chronic disorder that causes pain and stiffness throughout the tissues that support and move the bones and joints. Pain and localized tender points occur in the muscles, particularly those that support the neck, spine, shoulders, and hips. The disorder includes widespread pain, fatigue, and sleep disturbances
Fibrous Capsule	A tough wrapping of tendons and ligaments that surrounds the joint.
Flare	A period in which disease symptoms reappear or become worse
Genetic Marker	A specific tissue type or gene, similar to a blood type, that is passed on from parents to their children. Some genetic markers are linked to certain rheumatic diseases.
Immune Response	The reaction of the immune system against foreign substances. When this reaction occurs against substances or tissues within the body, it is called an autoimmune reaction.
Immune System:	A complex system that normally protects the body from infections. It combines groups of cells, the chemicals that control them, and the chemicals they release
Inflammation:	A characteristic reaction of tissues to injury or disease. It is marked by four signs: swelling, redness, heat and pain.
Joint:	A junction where two bones meet. Most joints are composed of cartilage, joint space, fibrous capsule, synovium, and ligaments.

Joint Space	The volume enclosed within the fibrous capsule and synovium
Ligaments:	Bands of cordlike tissue that connect bone to bone. Muscle: A structure composed of bundles of specialized cells that, when stimulated by nerve impulses, contract and produce movement.
Myopathies:	Inflammatory and non-inflammatory diseases of muscle.
Myositis	Inflammation of a muscle
Nonsteroidal Anti-Inflammatory Drugs (NSAIDs)	A group of drugs, such as aspirin and aspirin-like drugs, used to reduce inflammation that causes joint pain, stiffness, and swelling.
Raynaud's	A circulatory condition associated with spasms in the blood vessels of the fingers and toes causing them to change color. After exposure to cold, these areas turn white, then blue, and finally red
Remission	A period during which symptoms of disease are reduced (partial remission) or disappear (complete remission).
Sicca Syndrome	A condition manifested by dry eyes and dry mouth.
Sleep Disorder:	One in which a person has difficulty achieving restful, restorative sleep, very common in patients with fibromyalgia.

Synovium	A tissue that surrounds and protects the joints. It produces synovial fluid that nourishes and lubricates the joints.
Tender Points	Specific locations on the body that are painful, especially when pressed.
Tendons	Fibrous cords that connect muscle to bone.

Summary

The hardest thing about living with someone who suffers from fibromyalgia is that nothing you do will take the pain away, however, there are things you can do that will make life with fibro a little bit better and easier to tolerate.

Never ever make the person feel bad that they are in pain because it causes an inconvenience. For example: you have to cancel plans at the last minute, they look down and tired when you feel great. It's not fair when it affects your day.

Try to adjust to it instead of adding additional stress onto the person.

It's only normal that it will get you down at some point, it's hard to watch someone you love suffer.

You will from time to time get annoyed but make sure when you do, you are annoyed at the fibro and not at the person.

Reassure the person that you do care for them and a little time out is just to clear your head and re adjust.

Remember that things that are simple for you are not always so for the person with fibro, simple things like carrying bags from the shops, even light ones will have an effect on random muscles.

Do not expect the person to be able to do as much as you.

Slow your pace down often. Fibro causes fatigue and trying to keep up to a regular pace will cause the person to burn out.

Take time to have reassuring cuddles and rest, the feeling of being loved and cared for is a great tonic.

Be patient, your partner may have to walk slower as they are in pain or may become tired easily, they may get depressed or anxious and are likely to be forgetful. Help by writing things down or sending reminders.

Let your partner talk about their pain as often as they need to and more importantly listen.

Try to understand what they are going through and ask then to describe the pain in detail as you might be able to ease the pain. Remember your partner isn't moaning, they are just letting you know how they feel so you know what you are dealing with.

Learn about fibro. The more you know the more you will both benefits.

Accept that you cannot take the pain away but you might be able to help make their day more pleasant just by being there and being supportive.

Plan little things, mini celebrations, short breaks, future travel etc. so you both have good things to look forward to and make life worth living.

The most important thing to us as a couple is communication, don't be afraid to talk, don't bottle up feelings, talk things through, keeping things bottled up inside is a one-way street to misery for all concerned.

Moving Forward.

I hope that this book has helped in understanding the effects fibromyalgia has on all who live with it, the one with it and those around them and how with a positive outlook and the desire to try just simple steps life with fibro can improve.

I have said it before and will carry on saying it because I know how true it is, life with fibro does not have to be all doom and gloom, Lynn's positive outlook and willingness to try, coupled with support and understanding have meant our life together has become a journey not a constant burden, we enjoy good times and the bad times are fewer, further apart and less severe

Although we are all different, the one thing we have in common is the hope that one day a cure or at least an effective treatment will be found. Until then all we can do is work together to live the best life possible.

Nobody will ever claim it's easy but it can be done.

So, stay positive, look for the positives and don't be afraid to take the steps you decide you need to take, no matter how small, each one makes a difference.

Inspirational Quotes

The battle with fibromyalgia can be a lonely and frustrating one, to put it mildly. Finding the motivation to keep fighting in the face of daily pain and discomfort can seem impossible at times.

Here are some inspiring quotes from 'our little book of inspiration' to help keep you going in your battle with chronic pain:

"It does not matter how slowly you go as long as you do not stop" - Confucias

This is a great one to remember when it comes to treatments and lifestyle changes. More often than not, it will take a little bit of time and a lot of persistence before you notice any results. They key is to resist the initial urge to give up if you don't see immediate results. Stay with it, you'll be glad you did.

"Behind every chronic illness is just a person trying to find their way in the world. We want to find love and be loved and be happy just like you. We want to be successful and do something that matters. We're just dealing with unwanted limitations in our hero's journey." – Glenn Schweitzer

This is one I think is fantastic even though he talks about his Parkinsons it relates to any condition.

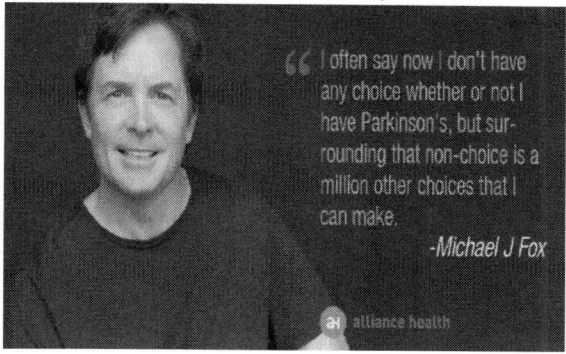

> I often say now I don't have any choice whether or not I have Parkinson's, but surrounding that non-choice is a million other choices that I can make.
> -Michael J Fox

"When you get to the end of your rope, tie a knot and hang on"- Franklin D Roosevelt

Everyone reaches the end of their rope sometimes.

When you feel overwhelmed and on the brink of caving in, step back, take a deep breath, close your eyes and tie an imaginary knot in an imaginary piece of rope and just hang on.
Ride out the storm as best you can and eventually, as Lynn always says "It will pass"

"Courage does not always roar. Sometimes courage is the quiet voice at the end of the day saying, 'I will try again tomorrow." – Mary Anne Radmacher

"Our greatest weakness lies in giving up. The most certain way to succeed is always to just try one more time." – Thomas Edison

"The measure of who we are is what we do with what we have." – Vince Lombardi

> **NOT EVERYTHING THAT IS FACED CAN BE CHANGED, BUT NOTHING CAN BE CHANGED UNTIL IT IS FACED.**
>
> — James Baldwin

Useful Products.

Over the years, Lynn has tried and tested many products, some have worked and some have not. Everyone is different and what may work for some may not work for others.

The trick is to source inexpensive products to try so that valuable funds are not wasted and also try things that work for others. After all the thing you have in common is fibromyalgia so many products that work for one person are likely to work for many.

We have dedicated a page on our website www.fibropartners.com which shows products that help Lynn that are inexpensive but effective. They vary from oils such as magnesium oil that Lynn trialed for a local company 3 years ago and still uses today, cbd oil (the sort that is legal in UK), various supports and also techniques that Lynn uses to relax.

So, please do visit the website, www.fibropartners.com and join us on our support group

https://www.facebook.com/groups/354657951343637/ for all the up to date information and support.

A MESSAGE TO PARTNERS

Your partners have Fibromyalgia; they would like your patience but most of all they need your understanding

When their faces are etched with pain

Don't ask "what's wrong with you?"

You know what's wrong, it's fibro.

When they can't walk at your pace, don't tell them "HURRY" just slow down and walk together, it's not a race

When fatigue means they have to back out of a social engagement at the last minute don't tell them they have spoilt your night.

Be their pillow and know what's best, stay home tonight and let them rest

When Fibro fog descends and they can't remember where things are, don't say "you are losing your mind"

Just take the time to help them find

If they say the same thing twice don't tell them they said that already

Just listen once then listen twice

Don't be harsh just be nice

If words get jumbled and make no sense

Just sort them out and don't get tense

This thing called Fibro is so demanding What really helps is

UNDERSTANDING.

Dedications and acknowledgements.

I would like to say a big thank you for the support from all the kind people who inspired and encouraged me to write this book.

Thank you to Danny Howard of 'Ambiactivate' for his tireless work in creating and maintaining our support website www.fibropartners.com and is help formatting this publication

I would like to dedicate this book, firstly to my wonderful partner Lynn, one of the bravest women I know with such a positive, never give up attitude and a willingness to continually work towards improvement with her condition.

I would also like to dedicate this book to all the other brave people who manage with fibromyalgia and indeed other chronic conditions.

You are all brave, strong individuals in the fight against fibromyalgia or any other chronic condition.

"You wake up every morning to fight the same demons that left you so tired the night before, and that, my love, is bravery."

I would like to also dedicate this book to a brave friend and admin on our fibropartners support group, Jennifer 'Jenny' Fore who was a great friend from across the ocean in the USA, who sadly passed away on June the 10th 2018. Jenny was always there to offer support and to listen, despite battling against fibromyalgia and other conditions.

R.I.P Jenny, sadly missed, loved by many and never to be forgotten.

She made broken look beautiful and strong look invincible. She walked with the universe on her shoulders and made it look like a pair of wings." – Ariana Dancu

Printed in Poland
by Amazon Fulfillment
Poland Sp. z o.o., Wrocław